Re-Thinking AD/HD

Re-Thinking AD/HD

A Guide for Fostering Success in Students with AD/HD at the College Level

Edited by **Patricia Quinn, M.D., and Anne McCormick, M. Ed.**

ADVANTAGE BOOKS

DEDICATIONS

For Patrick and for all high school seniors with ADD, so that when you are ready for college, college will be ready for you.

P.O.Q.

To my son, Ben, who has succeeded despite formidable odds, and is a model for the students I have had the privilege of working with for over 25 years. As he has achieved, may many of you.

A.McC.

Library of Congress Cataloging-in-Publication Data

Re-thinking AD/HD : a guide to fostering success in students with AD/HD at the college level / edited by Patricia Quinn and Anne McCormick.
p. cm.
Includes bibliographical references.
ISBN 0-9660366-3-8 (pbk.)
1. Attention-deficit-disordered youth--Education (Higher)--United States. 2. Attention-deficit hyperactivity disorder -- United States. 3. Learning disabled --Education (Higher)--United States. 4. College student orientation -- United States. I. Quinn, Patricia O. II. McCormick, Anne, 1947-
LC4713.4.R4 1998
371.92'6 -- dc21 98-38161
CIP

Cover design by Nelton Castro

Published by
ADVANTAGE BOOKS
4400 East-West Hwy.
Suite 816
Bethesda, Maryland 20814

Manufactured in the United States of America

10 9 8 7 6 5 4 3 2 1

Contents

Contributors

Loring Brinkerhoff, Ph.D., is employed by Educational Testing Service (ETS) as their disability accommodations specialist. He is also a higher education and disability consultant for Recording for the Blind & Dyslexic (RFB&D) and an adjunct professor of special education at Tufts University.

Jane Byron, M.A., is Director of Learning Disabilities Services, University of North Carolina, Chapel Hill. She has a B.S. in special education (Southern Connecticut University) and an M.A. in special education (College Programming for Students with LD, University of Connecticut, Storrs). Interests include the development of programming and campus-wide policies for college students with LD/ADHD.

Patrick J. Kilcarr, Ph.D., is Director of Georgetown University's Center for Personal Development. He is founder and executive director of the Georgetown Outdoor Leadership School (GOALS). Dr. Kilcarr received his Master's degree in Marriage and Family Therapy and a Doctorate in Developmental Psychology from the Institute for Child Study, University of Maryland, College Park.

Peter S. Latham, J.D., and Patricia H. Latham, J.D., are partners in the Washington, D.C., law firm Latham & Latham. They are founders and directors of the National Center for Law and Learning Disabilities (NCLLD), and arbitrators for the American Arbitration Association. They have coauthored seven books, contributed chapters to six additional books, and spoken extensively on learning disabilities, on AD/HD, and on legal issues in employment, licensing, and education. They are listed in *Who's Who in America*.

Anne McCormick, M.Ed., is Associate Director of Learning Services at American University. She began the Learning Services program for students with learning disabilities 15 years ago and is a frequent presenter at conferences on learning disabilities and attention deficit disorder.

David R. Parker, M.S., is Assistant Director of Learning Disabilities Services at the University of North Carolina at Chapel Hill. He has a B.S. in Education (Special Education, Indiana University) and an M.S. in Education (Counseling, Indiana University). Currently, David is Co-chair of the Learning Disabilities Special Interest Group for the Association on Higher Education and Disability (AHEAD). His special interests include program development, staff training, and addressing the psychosocial needs of college students with LD and AD/HD.

Patricia O. Quinn, M.D., is a Developmental Pediatrician in Washington, D.C. She received her M.D. degree from Georgetown University Medical School. Her pediatric training and a two-year fellowship in Child Development were completed at the Georgetown University Medical Center. Dr. Quinn has practiced exclusively in the areas of learning disabilities and attention deficit disorder and has contributed much to the field. She has authored or edited several books on these topics including **ADD and the College Student** and **Attention Deficit Disorder: Diagnosis and Treatment from Infancy to Adulthood.** She is a Clinical Assistant Professor of Pediatrics at Georgetown University.

Julie Sayer, B.A., graduated from Connecticut College in 1997 with a double major in psychology and child development. She wrote her psychology honors thesis on the validity and reliability of measurements used to diagnose AD/HD in adults. Currently, she works as a research assistant in the Pediatric Psychopharmacology Research Unit at Massachusetts General Hospital. She plans to attend graduate school in child psychology in 1999.

Lynne Shea, M.A., is an Associate Professor of English, Landmark College, in Putney, Vt., an institution exclusively serving those with specific learning disabilities. She is also Director of the Landmark College Women's Resource Center.

Helen Steinberg, M.S.Ed., has been Coordinator of the Learning Services Program at American University since 1986. She is a learning consultant with Georgetown Day School and in private practice in Washington, D.C. She has worked in the field of special education since 1972 as a resource teacher, supervisor of student teachers, and coordinator of an academic program for foster children. She serves on the Executive Board of the Washington, D.C. Branch of the International Dyslexia Association (IDA).

Paul Steinberg, M.D., is Associate Director of Georgetown University's Counseling and Psychiatric Service and is in private practice in Washington, D.C. In addition, he is associate clinical professor in the Department of Psychiatry at the George Washington University Medical Center and assistant clinical professor in the Department of Psychiatry, Georgetown University.

James Sydnor-Greenberg, Ph.D., is a Clinical Psychologist and Neuropsychologist in private practice in Falls Church, Va. He received his Ph.D. in clinical psychology from Catholic University, Washington D.C. He completed a clinical psychology internship and a neuropsychology post-doctoral fellowship at Harvard Medical School/Massachusetts Mental Health Center, and forensic training at the University of Virginia Institute of Law, Psychiatry, and Public Policy. He is Director of Psychology Services at Dominion Hospital, Falls Church, Va., and is Clinical Instructor, Department of Psychiatry, Georgetown University Medical Center.

Patrick Turnock, M.S., L.S.W., is an instructor of psychology at Wittenburg University, Wittenburg,Ohio, and a therapist at a residential treatment center in Ohio. He works primarily with adolescents with AD/HD and behavioral disorders. He completed his Master's degree at Colorado State University in Fort Collins, Co., where he is finishing his doctoral dissertation on coping among students with AD/HD.

Stuart A. Vyse, Ph.D., received his Ph.D. in school psychology at the University of Rhode Island, where he wrote his dissertation on the effects of methylphenidate on learning in children with attention deficit hyperactivity disorder. He is the author of **Believing in Magic: The Psychology of Superstition** (Oxford, 1997), and is Associate Professor of Psychology, Connecticut College, New London, Ct.

Preface

RE-THINKING AD/HD is a compilation of articles written in response to the unique needs of young adults with AD/HD who are attending college today in increasing numbers. Recent research on AD/HD supports the need for recognition and treatment for this segment of the postsecondary population. Educational programming for these students must, therefore, now include medical, psychological, and academic interventions to address all aspects of this complex disorder.

These developments demand reshaping of programming at the postsecondary level. It is becoming clear that we can no longer continue to serve these students under the umbrella of services and programming for students with learning disabilities. Universities are responding and beginning the process of change. **RE-THINKING AD/HD** discusses issues related to these changes and offers a model for colleges involved in adapting, designing, and implementing programming for students with AD/HD.

RE-THINKING AD/HD represents the collaboration of a wide range of professionals from the medical, psychological, and educational communities. It includes unique perspectives on issues of gender, medication, learning strategies, and health care needs among college students with AD/HD. Despite presenting such a broad perspective, **RE-THINKING AD/HD** continues to focus on how to implement new programming within the financial constraints facing most private colleges and universities. Collaboration with other student service providers on college campuses is proposed as a programming and service model to provide an inclusive program for students with AD/HD in a financially reasonable manner.

Yet, as the service provider's ability for referring students with AD/HD to appropriate programs increases, so does the need for adequate formal and informal diagnosis of the disability. Guidelines for documentation as developed by the Consortium on AD/HD Documentation are provided as a possible model for other programs. It remains, however, that issues pertaining to diagnosis and the psychological aspects of this diagnostic process must continue to be examined in depth.

One complicating factor in diagnosing AD/HD is its comorbidity with a host of other psychological conditions. **RE-THINKING AD/HD** addresses comorbidity factors from the service provider's perspective. Risks facing college students with AD/HD are discussed in candid articles on alcohol and substance abuse. Additional articles highlight the importance of including medication in the treatment plan for college students with AD/HD.

RE-THINKING AD/HD affirms the belief that students with AD/HD can succeed in spite of the challenges of the college experience and offers a model to foster this success.

Patricia O. Quinn, M.D.
Anne McCormick, M. Ed.

MOVING ALONG THE PROGRAMMING CONTINUUM: FROM LD TO AD/HD

Helen Steinberg, M.S.Ed.
Coordinator, Learning Services Program
American University

In the past five years, there has been a surge in the number of students with AD/HD appearing on college campuses. Typically, organization and time management are the weakest areas for these students. As a result, students with AD/HD are at great risk for being placed on probation or dropping out of college. Students with AD/HD require a different set of academic survival skills than those students diagnosed with learning disabilities. In order to meet the unique academic needs of students with AD/HD, learning counselors must engage these students by becoming more proactive and creative in their interventions. With ongoing support, students with AD/HD can, ultimately, become highly successful students.

In the late seventies, American University was one of the first universities to design and implement an academic support program to serve students with learning disabilities. Educational institutions were faced with the challenge of meeting the academic needs of bright and capable students who had been diagnosed with a variety of learning disabilities.

Although these deficits affected all academic domains, reading and writing were the two major skills interfering with students' educational achievement. Unless these students received academic support and educational accommodations, it would be a major challenge for them to reach their academic and professional goals.

In 1980, the Learning Services Program, a program for entering freshmen with documented learning disabilities, began serving these students. This program was a unique concept in that it was a structured, yet flexible, mainstream program. The key components included special sections of College Reading (study skills), three-day-a-week College Writing (freshmen English), and twice-weekly, one-on-one meetings with the coordinator of the program and other learning service counselors.

In 1990, a special section of Finite Math, which included a mentor /tutor, was added to the program. For the population of students with AD/HD applying to American University it was an ideal situation. Students desired mainstream education; parents were reassured that their children would not fall through the cracks if enrolled in the learning disabilities program.

The admissions office worked in tandem with Learning Services, and the coordinator of the program served on the admissions committee reviewing the applicants applying to the program. In addition to completing the regular application process, students completed a Supplementary Application and essay describing their learning disability. The essays reflected the academic frustration many of these students had experienced, particularly when there was a late diagnosis or lack of educational support. One applicant wrote:

> **I am not trying to live up to some 'ideal' standard. I am writing because academics are a struggle that I hope to conquer some day. Regardless of the degree of difficulty, nothing ever comes easily for me. I have had to reach out, grab it, hold on for dear life, and practice even more, until I perfect it. I am never satisfied. There is always more that can be done to improve.**

Another student wrote,

> **I finally thought I had conquered my problem but then high school arrived. My first year, I struggled, but still managed to get some decent grades. In my sophomore year, I hit an all time low and let my problem get the best of me.**

And put even more eloquently by another applicant,

> **"Puzzled, desperate, uncertain, frantic and helpless, and exhausted, are just some words that describe me while I am doing my school work. I get very frustrated with myself but I never give up.**

Although these students felt frustration, many persevered in their academic pursuits. This was reflected in the information submitted in their applications.

During the first twelve years of the Learning Services Program, the admissions committee reviewed thousands of applications from students with learning disabilities. Although there was some variation among students, they usually presented with similar academic profiles. In fact, most students presented fairly consistent grades of 3.0 or higher, while their SAT's, particularly the verbal section, was significantly lower.

The admissions committee believed that the SAT's were not a true reflection of the students' true potential. The majority of students applying to the program prior to 1992 reported problems with learning areas of reading, writing , and in some cases, math. Providing structured classes in reading, writing, and math seemed to be the perfect formula. It was apparent that with appropriate interventions, these students could have extremely successful undergraduate, graduate, and professional experiences.

Beginning in 1992 however, there was a sudden shift in the diagnoses of students applying to the Learning Services Program. In addition to reading comprehension and expressive language problems, a number of students were reporting the diagnosis of Attention Deficit Disorder. In reviewing the applications of these students, the admissions committee noted significant differences in their high school profiles and recommendations as compared to those students with "traditional" learning disabilities.

These differences included inconsistent grades in the same subject, poor performance in elective courses (e.g. physical education) and teacher reports detailing lack of motivation and follow-through. The academic profiles that students with AD/HD were presenting had more to do with application of skills rather than academic aptitude.

Initially, students applying to the Learning Services Program had described their frustration with school in terms of their academic skills rather than with issues of concentration, distractibility, hyperactivity, impulsivity, motivation and procrastination. The essays were powerful, emotional descriptions of the utter frustration and chaos that students with AD/HD had experienced both socially and educationally. Nothing describes the pain and confusion that these students were experiencing than to quote from their personal experiences. An applicant wrote the following:

> **My learning disability was diagnosed during my junior year. I had experienced a great deal of frustration in school during my first two years of high school. I also began to suspect that I might have attention deficit disorder because I was having problems paying attention to my work. I tried very hard to perform well on my final exams, and did very poorly. Due to my efforts and poor exam grades, my mom thought that I should be evaluated. I was relieved to learn that I had ADD, and that I was not just a lazy, stupid kid. The biggest impact on my school performance has been the recognition that I have ADD. I began taking Ritalin and the effect of the medication was immediate. I have been an honor roll student with a B average since taking medication. I think the medication has had the greatest impact on my schoolwork. The support from my family and school has allowed me to become the student I always knew I could be.**

By 1992, the educational profile of students applying to the Learning Services Program had shifted dramatically from students presenting fairly consistent grades, or at least an upward trend, to students having transcripts with peaks and valleys. There was no particular explanation as to why students' grades went from B's to D's, or C's to A's. In addition, the admissions committee noticed a pattern of poor performance in elective courses, appearing to be more a reflection of effort and attitude rather than aptitude. Many of these students were enrolled in Honors and/or A.P. classes.

In other words, these students had the potential to be successful students, but something significant was interfering with their academic success. In fact, students diagnosed with AD/HD had academic profiles opposite of students diagnosed with "pure" learning disabilities (skills).

The admissions committee now had the mission of reviewing applications of students with higher SAT's/ACT's and very unpredictable grades. The GPA's of these students was often below 2.5, with the average around 2.3. The university was faced with the challenge of making admissions decisions for a new group of students seeking college admission into a competitive university. A prospective student wrote:

> **My teachers called me lazy, my friends said I had no control. Administrators labeled me bright, but uninterested - able, but undisciplined. Given the attention and focusing difficulties that I was experiencing, my school work was marked by inconsistencies, poor performance, frustration and failure. When I recall the great anxiety that has dominated my academic career, I am still saddened. As an active little girl in**

elementary school, I was continually reprimanded by my teachers for my inability to concentrate and focus on the tasks at hand. Not until the end of my junior year in high school was I diagnosed with Attention Deficit Disorder. Instead of being frightened by the diagnosis, I was relieved. At last, I knew the conditions from which I suffered could be improved. Since identification, the situation has changed dramatically. Hopefully, now that I am able to concentrate more effectively, all educational areas will begin to reflect what I consider to be my strong intellectual potential. In all, I am aware of my problems and am committed to learning to compensate for them.

For the first time in my educational career, I anticipate a decidedly successful school year and expect my grades to reflect my new found acceptance of both my disabilities and myself. I know that I can be an asset to American University and am eager to become a member of the Class of 1993.

In addition, the high school college counselors were writing recommendations that reflected the problems that these students were facing. The following college recommendation describes the positive outcome that can occur when the symptoms of AD/HD are recognized and intervention follows:

There have been two Karen Smiths at Stonehill. The 'old' Karen often felt stupid, frustrated, and therefore, unmotivated. The 'new' Karen is eager to learn, a good problem-solver and has learned to take the initiative to work with her teachers. The old Karen nearly left Stonehill; the new Karen will graduate gracefully in May. What a pleasure to see this transformation. At the point when Karen was considering leaving Stonehill, her parents had her evaluated. The underlying problem was Attention Deficit Disorder. Learning this about herself changed Karen's outlook. The new Karen emerged, self-confidence grew, and she worked to develop new coping strategies.

During the past six years, the number of students diagnosed with AD/HD either attentive or inattentive type, with and without learning disabilities, has increased significantly. Keeping in mind that the original mission of the Learning Services Program was designed for students with learning disabilities, we, at American University, and at colleges and universities across the country, have had to adapt to the specific needs of this particular population.

No longer was the addition of a special section of College Reading, Writing or Math and additional tutoring going to be sufficient for students with AD/HD. The typical accommodations of additional time for exams, use of the computer, books on tape, and/or a reader or scribe were not necessarily the accommodations that would provide what this very distinct group of students required in order to be successful students.

Flexible and creative programming has been the key to working with students with AD/HD. Professionals providing support in academic centers on college campuses agree that this population of students is at the greatest risk for failure. Why is this the case?

College does not provide the ongoing external structure that is essential for students with AD/HD, particularly if they are not responsive to or have not been prescribed medication. It is the first time that these students have jumped overboard without someone throwing them a lifeline. After years of parental nagging, teacher reminders, and daily contact with peers, suddenly these students are thrust into an environment foreign to them.

Now, it is solely their responsibility to be punctual for class, structure each day, keep track of their syllabi and ongoing assignments, plan ahead, buy their textbooks and materials, organize their room, remember to eat and sleep, initiate communication with their professors, navigate their way across campus to their classes, figure out the library system, engage socially with strangers, and assess when they need help and to whom to turn.

These are just some of the tasks that all college students must handle. However, when one's "inner clock" is not working and time has no meaning, in addition to distractibility, impulsivity, attentional and memory deficits, each one of these tasks is a challenge.

All too often, when students with AD/HD are asked to fill in a blank 168-hour/week schedule, they are in disbelief when asked to account for their time. They honestly do not know where the hours and days have gone.

They do know that the time has not been invested in studying. For some students, these tasks become so overwhelming that they often tune out and become academically paralyzed. It is for this reason that we must build into our academic centers programming to meet the needs of students with AD/HD.

The Learning Services Program at American University has sustained its initial mission in meeting the needs of students with learning disabilities for almost 18 years. However, the admissions office and learning services center presently receive hundreds of calls requesting information regarding our program for students with AD/HD. Although the essential ingredients for success are in place for students with AD/HD, additional approaches have been instituted to meet the needs of these students.

Unlike students with learning disabilities, students with AD/HD must address their medication needs prior to their arrival on a college campus. If indicated, psychostimulant medication should be prescribed by a physician or psychiatrist while the student is still living at home. The student benefits from experimenting with the appropriate dosage and optimal scheduling while being monitored by family members and teachers.

For the first time, letters will be sent from our office to those students who self-identified during the admissions process. In order to lessen the stress making the transition from high school to college, it is suggested that students consider a medication evaluation before entering school. We view this as an essential proactive step on the part of the student and the university.

Once the student arrives on campus, it is imperative that he/she meet with a learning counselor to help with organizational and time-management skills. Academic contracts work exceedingly well, especially daily phone contacts. Voice-mail is an ideal method for students to inform their counselor of progress.

Designing individual plans in which the student is invested requires flexibility, a sense of humor, and an awareness of the high degree of frustration these students may be experiencing. For example, many students don't use their day-planners because they say that they forget to look at it. Instead, they write their important assignments and appointments on their hands because it will be with them at all times. As a result, the names of learning counselors are often advertised on the hands of many students across campus.

Counseling and academic support centers should work closely with students concerning use of psychostimulant medications. Learning counselors can arrange regularly scheduled meetings focusing on time management and organization. Students can be assisted in taking greater responsibility for their behavior by using academic contracts and follow-up phone calls. College students with AD/HD need on-going assistance to organize their lives and structure their environment.

Although progress has been made in diagnosing students with AD/HD, more must be done to enable these capable students to have successful college careers. Some strategies should begin well before the student enters college , while more structured programming should be considered by the academic support center at the college.

Early intervention should include communication between students, parents, teachers, and counselors, and must begin as soon as the student is diagnosed. By including the student in parent-teacher conferences, he/she learns to be accountable and more responsible for his/her behavior. Written goals can serve to clarify for all involved what is expected of each participant. Although it may be difficult for parents to step aside as their child struggles to attain these set goals, it can be an extremely positive experience for the student as he/she accomplishes a particular task on his/her own. Taking personal responsibility is critical for success in college.

On the continuum of programming for students with learning disabilities, in addition to serving students with traditional learning disabilities, learning service counselors are screening an increased number of students with AD/HD. Currently, it appears that no specific program has been designed to meet the specific needs of these students. Where do we go from here?

The ideal academic support program for students with AD/HD would be 24-hour monitoring in a structured living situation. Short of that, creative and proactive programming may include medication monitoring, daily phone or e-mail communication, regularly scheduled meetings with an academic counselor, communication with professors, and written contracts setting clear goals. Flexibility and creativity are crucial factors in working with students with AD/HD in college. In order to have success, individual needs must be assessed and, most importantly, the student must be invested and "buy" into the program.

As Karen's college counselor stated at the end of his recommendation:

> **We have seen Karen grow from a frustrated, tired child into and upbeat, self-confident young woman. Obviously, the process is not yet finished, but so far the results have been dramatic. I concur with her advisor that the best is yet to come; we give Karen our enthusiastic recommendation.**

Karen was admitted to American University and after almost three years of on-going support, she is on her way to graduating with honors.

□

DIFFERENCES BETWEEN COLLEGE STUDENTS WITH AD/HD AND LD: PRACTICAL IMPLICATIONS FOR SERVICE PROVIDERS

David R. Parker, M.S., and Jane Byron, M.A.
Learning Disabilities Services
University of North Carolina at Chapel Hill

A rapid increase in university students with AD/HD led a comprehensive learning disabilities (LD) program to reevaluate its effectiveness in identifying and responding to the needs of these new students. An extensive self-study allowed the program's LD specialists to refine their understanding of the impact that AD/HD can have on college students, and how these difficulties differ from those that are typically encountered by college students with LD. This article summarizes key learnings from this evaluation process and describes specific changes made to the LD program's service delivery model.

INTRODUCTION

Learning Disabilities Services (LDS), at the University of North Carolina at Chapel Hill, provides accommodations and services to currently-enrolled students with learning disabilities (LD), attention deficit disorders (AD/HD), and traumatic brain injuries (TBI). Undergraduate and graduate students alike must submit current documentation of their disability and its educational impact in order to become eligible to work with the office. The mission of LDS is to assist students in achieving their academic potential within the regular academically competitive university curriculum.

The LDS program model was based on the research and examples of "best practices" in the field of college programming for LD students. A strong component of this model was the ability to offer learning strategies instruction. Like many other college programs for students with LD, LDS endorsed strategies instruction as an essential component of its program model (Anderson, 1998) and, in doing so, embraced the "spirit of the law."

Philosophically, the office was committed to helping students develop greater independence as learners and to teach them specific skills they could use and accommodations to develop their intellectual potential.

An extensive body of research supported the view that many college students with LD were strategy-deficient (Brinckerhoff, Shaw, & McGuire, 1993). Widespread practice has shown that direct instruction with time for modeling, guided practice, and on-going evaluation as the student generalized the skill, contributed to the success and independence of adult learners with LD (Crux, 1991).

While the mission and philosophy of the office have not changed, trends of the past three years have led the staff to reexamine how well their program model meets the needs of students with AD/HD. These trends helped LD specialists at LDS develop a greater understanding of differences in educational impact of LD and AD/HD. Until fairly recently, these two disabilities were seen as similar information-processing deficits. Professional training in the field of learning disabilities reinforced this view. They offered one program model which they felt met equally well the needs of college students with both of these disabilities.

College students with LD and AD/HD share enough issues to make LD specialists ideally suited for meeting the needs of both groups. This was particularly relevant at LDS, where students with AD/HD sought out services (including strategies instruction) as frequently as did students with LD. However, there are enough differences between the impact of AD/HD and LD to warrant a need for all service providers, including LD specialists, to retool with new skills and knowledge.

On a broader scale, the rapid growth in numbers of college students with AD/HD may lead other service providers to reevaluate the effectiveness of their current services for students with this disability. Two questions are addressed in this article:

1) How do the needs of college students with AD/HD differ from the needs of college students with LD?

(2) How did a comprehensive LD program adapt its program model to respond to these emerging needs?

EVALUATING THE EFFECTIVENESS OF AN LD PROGRAM MODEL

In recent years, the number of students with AD/HD eligible to use LDS has shown a consistent increase. In the spring of 1998, students with this disability made up nearly 60% of the total number of students eligible to work with this office. In 1992, only 18% of the population of students who were eligible to use LDS had been diagnosed with ADD or AD/HD. Similar growth rates are being reported on many other campuses (Nadeau, 1995). A number of factors appear to be contributing to this trend:

- The first generation of students identified as AD/HD in K to 12 schooling is now matriculating to college. Many of these students (and their parents) are knowledgeable about their educational rights and are proactive about seeking accommodations and services. This parallels a 20-year trend with college students with LD.
- Increased media attention to AD/HD has led to an increase in referrals (often self-referrals) for diagnostic testing.
- Diagnosing professionals are rapidly developing more sophisticated approaches to making an accurate diagnosis, including the ability to differentially diagnose AD/HD from other "look alike" disorders.
- Some college programs for students with LD are beginning to publicize services for students with AD/HD, too. In most cases, these are identical services. The most

recent edition of *Colleges with Programs for Students with Learning Disabilities or Attention Deficit Disorders* (Mangrum and Strichart, 1997), for example, now includes specific listings for students with AD/HD.

- The educational, medical, and therapeutic communities now recognize that many children do not "outgrow" AD/HD. Again, this trend has a similar antecedent in the field of LD.

- The field of AD/HD is coming into its own, separate from the field of LD. Today, conferences, electronic listservs, publications, and support groups abound for adults with AD/HD.

On the University of North Carolina at Chapel Hill campus, students with AD/HD and LD could access the same strategies instruction and could *request* the same accommodations. As students with AD/HD began to present their requests to LDS in growing numbers, limitations of an LD-based program model began to emerge. Last year, the authors reported that students and staff members alike began identifying these limitations as a mismatch between students' needs and the program's services (Byron and Parker, 1997). Examples of this poor fit are described below.

> **Staff members were unclear about students' academic needs.**

Unlike LD assessment reports, most of the AD/HD assessment reports presented by students contained minimal information about the impact of their disability in a college setting. These reports made no recommendations about appropriate accommodations/services or they made sweeping conclusions (e.g., "This student cannot learn a foreign language.") without adequate supporting data.

During initial meetings with these students, LDS staff members often encountered more questions than answers. First, limited understanding of the impact of AD/HD made it difficult for LD specialists to ask the right questions or to fully understand what students reported. Second, students with AD/HD often found it difficult to summarize their disability-related needs. Students with LD are more likely to come to college with a history of an earlier diagnosis as well as prior experience with accommodations and/or services.

These students can draw upon this history to identify ways in which their disability affects them once they are in college. They often know a great deal about the accommodations and services they will need. This is not to say that students with LD find the transition from high school to college easy. A growing number of students with AD/HD, however, have even less experience to draw upon once they are aware of their need for accommodations or services in a postsecondary setting.

Students with AD/HD often have later dates of initial diagnosis and less history with accommodations and services prior to college. In the Spring of 1998, for example, 62% of students with AD/HD who actively used LDS were diagnosed for the first time in college. This figure contrasted sharply with students with LD. During the same semester, only 5% of students with this disability who actively used LDS were diagnosed for the first time in college.

> **Students found it difficult to develop and follow through on plans.**

As recently as two years ago, LD staff members developed an Individualized Academic Plan (IAP) with each student who utilized LDS. This was a semester-long plan that identified services and accommodations the office would provide the student. Developing an IAP entailed: asking the student to prioritize his/her needs for the semester; identifying the impact of the student's disability in his/her classes; formulating a long-range intervention plan; and then implementing that plan in a fairly linear fashion from one weekly session to another.

Difficulties prioritizing, planning and follow-through often were the core disabling conditions encountered by students with AD/HD. Many students found it difficult to identify their needs or to anticipate the barriers they might encounter as they pursued their goals. Nonetheless, LDS staff members helped students with AD/HD develop IAP's and then tried to follow these plans over the course of the semester.

The LD specialists began to realize how difficult this process could be for a student who tended to live "in the moment" without effective problem-solving skills. Staff members found themselves starting sessions with the last topic addressed in the previous session, only to learn that the student had already implemented a solution or now wanted to focus on a new issue. Unlike many students with LD, students with AD/HD frequently encountered a myriad of new difficulties during the week between sessions.

Students' difficulties with "sticking to the plan" also emerged during their sessions at LDS. Some students with AD/HD found it difficult to focus on any one topic long enough to address it completely. They would shift to another topic without monitoring or redirecting their own thought process. They would forget important issues they had wanted to address in their sessions. Many students preferred to talk about their frustrations and academic difficulties but found it difficult to implement any solutions by making changes in their behavior.

Because staff members respected the student's right to set his/her own agenda, they initially tried to be flexible with students' spontaneous agendas. This approach presented its own problems. Staff members felt poorly prepared to conduct productive meetings. They found it difficult to monitor a student's progress over the course of a semester. Some students began to report low satisfaction levels with what they were accomplishing in their sessions at LDS and expressed frustration with their own lack of focus and structure.

When LDS service providers evaluated student frustrations, they asked themselves if strategies instruction was the most appropriate solution to many of these students' needs. In case after case, it seemed as if students with AD/HD already possessed effective academic skills but found it difficult to use them, especially on their own. **Time management** was the strategy area that began to highlight this distinction . Students with AD/HD frequently requested help with this strategy and demonstrated chronic time management problems more often than did their peers with LD.

The LD specialists initially attempted to teach students with AD/HD the same time management strategies that often helped students with LD. Usually this work centered on use of a calendar to develop, in advance, a long-range action plan. Students were taught how to establish deadlines, break down tasks, anticipate the amount of time needed to complete each task, and how to record this plan on a calendar.

These sessions would end with the student having a detailed, written plan for organizing the week, month, or even semester. Many students with AD/HD were already well-versed in these strategies. They showed the LD specialists various calendar systems and software that they had tried to use, however, without success.

In some cases, these students could **plan** their time when they stopped to think about it, but they had on-going difficulties **carrying out their plans** on their own. Other students with AD/HD became overwhelmed by a large project because they lacked the ability to prioritize a starting point. Students with both types of time management problems would procrastinate, thereby exacerbating the problem.

They would divert their attention to other tasks. They would become overwhelmed by the details of a task and spend far too much time on those details, only to realize too late that they had run out of time for completing the rest of the project. Students would come to their next session at LDS embarrassed and frustrated. They were usually at a loss to explain their inability to carry out the plan that had seemed so clear to them in their last session. Given the tremendous verbal intelligence that many of these students had, and their success in other areas of their life, the LD service providers initially found it difficult to understand students' problems in this area, too.

➢ **Staff members had questions beyond the student's academic needs.**

As the staff at LDS began to see more students with AD/HD, they realized that many of these students were involved in multimodal treatment plans. It became apparent that a high percentage of these students were taking prescription medications to manage their AD/HD. During the spring semester of 1998, for example, 75% of the students with AD/HD who actively used the LDS office were using stimulants, antidepressants, or both (compared to only 7% of students with LD who actively used the office). Until fairly recently, there were still many questions about use of medications by adults with this disability. A number of students began to report problems with their medications.

Some students, who continued to follow the same prescription they first received as children, worried about the effectiveness of their current dose. Students also began asking for information about new medications coming onto the market, such as Adderall. Some students struggled to recall, and succinctly summarize, their experiences with medications when they met with their doctors. The LD specialists were confronted with their own questions when they began to hear that Ritalin was becoming an abuse substance of choice on college campuses.

All of these concerns were compounded by students' transition to college. For many, college was the first time that they were solely dependent upon themselves to take their medications. This presented real challenges to some students with significant memory and organizational problems. As so often happens during students' transition to college, it was simply expected that they would suddenly be able to do this on their own. Staff and students alike had many questions about these medications issues.

Staff members also began to see that a large number of students had comorbid psychological diagnoses. Many were in therapy or on medications, or both, for depression, anxiety, and other affective disorders. In some cases, it was difficult for students to benefit from LDS services because these issues were not effectively being treated. These students tried unsuccessfully to carry out decisions and solutions they had reached during their sessions at LDS. They frequently experience chronic anxiety and organizational chaos that resisted successful academic intervention. At times, these students required immediate psychological care because of the emotional crisis they were in. While a significant number of college students with LD experienced psychosocial difficulties, these concerns were less severe and could often be addressed by LD service providers (Price, 1993).

Initially, as the number of students with AD/HD began to grow, the LDS staff drew upon their training in this area to try to understand and respond. However, the nature and severity of affective disorders in the AD/HD population exceeded the scope of treatment of psychosocial issues in the LD literature.

Recognizing that they were actually serving students with two different disabilities, an exciting challenge emerged. Now was the time to contact other service providers, read more about current interventions and, just as importantly, talk with the experts who were in the LDS office: the students with AD/HD. The timing was right because the field of adults with AD/HD was exploding with new information. Helpful resources were found both internally and externally.

The LDS staff first turned to valuable resources they could access within their office. One was Adults with Attention Deficit Disorders Listserv, on which adults with this disability generously shared their experiences, frustrations, and suggestions with a wider audience. The listserv provided a broader perspective on the experiences that students at LDS were reporting. Staff members learned more about medications and therapeutic issues. They also learned of new literature, conferences, and speakers. They read a rapidly growing number of books and articles on issues related to adults with AD/HD. These learning experiences helped the LD specialists clarify what they wanted to learn from students and gave them an invaluable context for understanding the real significance of what students were already telling them.

The National Attention Deficit Disorder Association (ADDA) conference provided direct contact with leaders in the field and findings from their research and practice. Both the sessions and the informal interactions with adults with AD/HD at the conference solidified the differences between LD and AD/HD that LDS staff members were beginning to see more clearly in their sessions with students.

LDS staff also networked with ADD coaches in private practice. Several students who used LDS introduced the staff to these coaches. They shared some of their techniques as well as their insights about the nature of this disability. LDS staff members began to explore the possibility of adapting some of these coaching techniques to their own work. For example, these early contacts demonstrated that coaches were very direct but in a manner that allowed students to provide their own answers.

Coaches helped students focus on tangible, short-term steps as opposed to long-range, detailed plans. Finally, coaches helped students implement plans once the session was over. The LD specialists were intrigued by the effectiveness they witnessed in the coaches' work. Their skills seemed uniquely matched to the impact of the student's disability. They decided to learn more from coaches and brought in national coaching experts from the American Coaching Association as consultants. They provided initial training, resource materials, and support while the staff explored how they could adapt relevant aspects of the coaching model.

On a national scale, there were countless discussions with other service providers in the field. Many of the staff members' questions focused on documentation guidelines and growth rates in the numbers of students with AD/HD on other campuses. Few colleagues could be found who were also adapting the coaching model for use in college; those who were doing this work had many of the same questions that the LDS staff members were exploring.

Thankfully, the field of adults with AD/HD was moving ahead with new research and implications for practice. This was happening at the same time that the field of postsecondary disability services was beginning to explore this topic, too. A pioneering resource that bridges the gap between these two fields is the *Journal of Postsecondary Education and Disability* (Spring/Fall 1995).

On campus, LDS staff reached out to other colleagues as well as students. Psychiatrists in the Student Health Center and psychologists in the University Counseling Center provided invaluable feedback and shared their concerns about effective multimodal treatment. Stronger referral procedures for both assessment and treatment were developed with these offices. Another informative source was an annual LDS evaluation by students. Results showed that many students with AD/HD felt that their disability-related needs could be met more effectively. A final, important source of learning was formation of a Quality Development Team. The LD specialists worked with key campus administrators, faculty members, and a student representative over several months to solicit feedback about services at LDS. This process included student surveys and focus groups, some of which specifically addressed questions about serving students with AD/HD.

All of these learning experiences resulted in a clearer understanding of the nature of AD/HD for LDS staff. Russell Barkley's theory provided a useful framework for thinking about this disability. Barkley, an Ad/Hd expert, hypothesized that people with AD/HD experience difficulty using three types of inhibition. This **dis**inhibition reduces the person's ability to use his/her executive functions to control his/her goal-directed behavior. Two of the four executive functions that are particularly impaired in the AD/HD mind are nonverbal and verbal working memory. He concluded that people with AD/HD are less able to use self-control as an effective method for regulating their own behavior in the moment and for directing their behavior to some future goal (Barkley, 1997).

Barkley distinguishes this disabling condition from a learning disability by naming AD/HD as a deficit in performance, not skills. As he said,

> **The totality of the deficits associated with AD/HD serve to cleave thought from action, knowledge from performance, past and future from the moment, and the dimension of time from the rest of the three-dimensional world more generally. This, as I have said before, means that AD/HD is not a disorder of knowing what to do, but of doing what one knows. It produces a disorder of applied intelligence by partially dissociating the crystallized intelligence of prior knowledge from its application in the day-to-day stream of adaptive functioning. AD/HD, then, is a disorder of performance more than a disorder of skill: a disability more in the "when" and "where" and less in the "how" or "what" of behavior. Those with AD/HD often know what they should do or should have done, but this provides little consolation to them, little influence over their behavior, and often much irritation to others (**pp. 15-16).

On a day-to-day basis, the LD specialists at LDS began to see more clearly how AD/HD could impact a student's academic experiences. Some of these areas of impact are described in the following paragraphs.

➢ **Difficulties with performance, not skills:** Students with AD/HD often possess academic strategies that may be lacking in college students with LD. The more prevailing impact of AD/HD, as summarized by Barkley, is often found in the student's inability to access these skills on demand and continue to implement them over time. LDS staff learned that they needed to teach students how to use their skills to carry out their plans. This often entailed helping the student develop "in-the-moment " reminders and prompts.

It also meant helping students learn to focus on one short-term goal that they could accomplish. Frequently, their thoughts would jump from one possibility to another. Such tangential thinking can be helpful in some situations (such as brainstorming or giving multiple directions simultaneously), but it often leads to procrastination when the student is trying to accomplish a previously planned task.

➢ **Difficulty with sustained attention:** Students with AD/HD can find it difficult to create and follow a cogent academic agenda for a session with a service provider. While students with LD are able to focus on one strategy area at a time, LD specialists at LDS learned they needed to work with students with AD/HD to structure a session differently. They frequently needed to focus on smaller goals. Students needed direct feedback when they began to pursue a different agenda from the one they had identified as important. Some students benefited from briefer sessions or "sessions" conducted over the phone or via e-mail.

➢ **Memory deficits are a frequent concern:** Students with AD/HD often report chronic short-term memory deficits. This impairment produces many consequences, including difficulty drawing upon their own histories to remember past successes/solutions, and the specific problem of remembering their train of thought while speaking. Students with AD/HD have a greater need than students with LD to have external reminders in their environment to compensate for this. LDS staff members often needed to provide such reminders, at least initially, during their sessions with students.

➢ **Attending during academic tasks:** Many students with LD request strategies to compensate for language-processing deficits. Sometimes, they repeatedly use the same strategy even when it's ineffective, rather than learning a new approach. In contrast, students with AD/HD seek strategies for staying focused while engaging in academic tasks such as reading or writing.

They typically do not encounter language-processing deficits and often take the risk of trying a novel approach. Students with AD/HD often reported this type of problem with attention in their math and foreign language classes. Conceptually, they can master the academic content, but attention to details and deficits in sequential memory result in "careless" errors when students with AD/HD sit down and do repetitive examples of this work on paper.

➢ **Related treatment options are the norm:** A high percentage of students with AD/HD use medications and/or therapy to address comorbid issues. While college students with LD frequently grapple with psychosocial issues, the presence of diagnosed affective disorders appears to be much lower in this group than students with AD/HD. Service providers at LDS were more likely to encounter barriers to successful work with students with AD/HD when these issues were not addressed. As a result, LDS staff communicated with other professionals who were working with these students (with their permission, of course) much more frequently compared to students with LD.

DEVELOPING A MORE EFFECTIVE PROGRAM MODEL

In order to address the limitations of their LD-based model, the LDS staff added more methods for clarifying the needs of students with AD/HD and for helping them develop performance-based skills. This section will describes specific changes made in their program model such as AD/HD documentation guidelines, a new intake process, and direct services for students with this disability.

Documentation Guidelines

As LDS service providers developed a better understanding of AD/HD, they found their old documentation guidelines failed to report important information. Previously, staff members at LDS, as well as service providers on many campuses, would accept a hand-scribbled note from a physician saying, in effect, "This student has ADD." LDS staff worked with colleagues from other state university campuses, as well as a representative from the state Vocational Rehabilitation Office, to create a new verification form that matches the format of the AD/HD criteria outlined in the Diagnostic and Statistical Manual (DSM-IV). This new document asks the diagnostician to endorse the specific criteria that the student meets. It also asks for brief information about medications and recommendations for therapy. This information was collected with the student's signed consent.

As knowledge in the field of assessment and treatment expanded, the limited information on this form became quickly inadequate. It was difficult to determine appropriate services and accommodations with such scanty documentation. The checklist didn't provide details about the current educational impact of the student's AD/HD, nor did it provide useful information about any comorbid issues. Finally, the form failed to address accommodations and services either by reporting on the student's educational history, or by making recommendations for current educational interventions. The LDS staff concluded that more helpful documentation would need to:

➢ be current, comprehensive and meet DSM-IV criteria;

➢ provide family, educational, medical, psychological and vocational histories;

➢ summarize outcomes of educational assessment, including aptitude testing (this was deemed to be critically important in order to rule out learning disabilities and to provide psychoeducational guidance in determining individualized accommodations and services);

➢ report on the assessment of the student's psychosocial functioning when indicated;

➢ and offer an interpretive summary and recommendations for services and/or accommodations that were supported by the findings of the report.

The authors have worked with campus colleagues and incorporated new national models to develop revised AD/HD documentation guidelines to meet these criteria.

Intake Process

Until more comprehensive assessment reports could be obtained, the LDS staff developed an intake process to supplement the dearth of information available in most students' AD/HD documentation. Students now are asked to complete and return an Intake Form prior to meeting with the Director or staff. Students' written responses, and what they discuss during the intake meeting, help to clarify their current needs, their levels of self-awareness, and clarify other treatments .

Staff members learn a great deal, about students' educational histories. In most cases, intake sessions confirm that these students have many strategies but find it difficult to use them effectively on demand. Current medications are recorded, and compliance and side-effect issues discussed. Similarly, information about therapy and other interventions (e.g., yoga, journaling, working with a private ADD coach) used by students is collected and recorded.

An unintended benefit of intake meetings is the powerful nature of the interaction itself. Many students have been diagnosed recently, or are seeking accommodations and services for the first time, or both. Therefore, these meetings often are one of the first times these students have a candid conversation with a caring professional about their disability, after their diagnosis. Many students express great deal of relief when discovering someone who understands their difficulties. They are pleasantly surprised to learn that staff members appreciate their strengths and work with other students who share some of their characteristics.

Many intake meetings have led to referrals for additional assessment, reinforcing staff member's belief that new guidelines, requiring educational testing will prove time-efficient for students, and add to understanding of strengths and weaknesses as learners. Educational assessment helps to focus on two accommodations meriting new interest for students with AD/HD: extended test time and taped textbooks. Many other campuses are also exploring these accommodations questions.

If a student with AD/HD is on medication and takes his/her exam in a separate test room, is extended test time necessary to "level the playing field"? With taped texts, service providers are asking: Is this accommodation appropriate for a student with adequate decoding skills but whose attentional deficits result in low comprehension or retention?

Additional time and experience will be needed to reach clear answers for these questions. LDS service providers believe that psychoeducational testing will play an important role in forming empirically based conclusions to these questions.

Direct Services

As the numbers of students with AD/HD have increased , their requests for **strategies instruction** has also. Initially, these students requested help primarily with time management and test-preparation strategies. Unlike many students with LD, they did not request a great deal of assistance with reading strategies or written language strategies. New ways to teach time-management skills have been designed. LDS staff members have learned that some students with AD/HD become overwhelmed when an entire project is task-analyzed into a myriad of steps. When working with these students, the LD specialists will instead, help them prioritize the most important tasks they are willing to complete in the immediate future.

Private ADD coaches taught LDS staff that some students needed to start with "baby steps." For example, a student beginning a research project might buy a notebook for organizing all the materials he/she will generate while writing the paper. A concrete starting point can help the student get started. He/she can begin to build a new history of success to replace a previous history of procrastination and organizational chaos.

Staff members also help some students evaluate the time and place in which they can be the most productive. This entails evaluating peak response periods to the student's medication as well as other parts of the day (such as immediately after exercise) when the student anticipates being more focused. Many alternative approaches to time management include some form of accountability on the student's part. Student and staff member form an alliance identifying comfortable ways for the student to follow-up on his/her progress that is realistic given the staff member's schedule. Usually, the student leaves an e-mail or voicemail message for the staff member. Follow-up might mean meeting two or three times a week for 15 minutes, instead of the previous "standard" schedule of one weekly session lasting 50 minutes.

Some students' difficulties with test preparation skills are secondary to their time -management problems. They demonstrate an "all or nothing" approach to scheduling their time to study for exams: they either find themselves procrastinating until the last minute, or they compulsively pour over class materials well past a level of sufficient mastery. Problems with saliency (i.e., being able to discern what is most important) can contribute to students' frustrations when preparing for tests.

They find it difficult to determine key points to focus on while studying. As a result, some students try to commit everything to memory, while others gamble that the material that they find interesting will be the focus of their exam. Finally, many students with AD/HD express difficulty preparing for exam formats that require convergent thinking. When tested using an essay format, for example, their grasp of concepts and their ability to perceive multiple connections between topics works in their favor.

When allowed to think divergently on these exams, they may sidestep difficulties with confrontational memory by thinking of another way to describe that part of their answer. When given multiple choice exams many students with AD/HD are frustrated by knowing the material but not being able to generate the correct answer. They report being able to justify several possible answers to a question, but are confused if the wording in a potential answer deviates from what they have committed to memory.

LDS staff members are helping students develop strategies for these problems, and to teach them to students with AD/HD in a way that acknowledges their attentional characteristics. Some strategies are similar to those that work with students with LD. LD specialists help students understand how their disability contributes to academic barriers. They help students develop new approaches

"Inspiration" software (Inspiration Software, Inc., 1997) helps students create a visual summary of text on the computer screen. The student easily can diagram this information into greater levels of detail so that on one screen, for example, only the main ideas are seen but on the next screen, the subpoints of any one of those main ideas are shown.

LDS staff members also facilitate 3-way meetings with interested students and instructors to help the student explain disability-related difficulties during exams. Some of these meetings lead instructors to change the format of their exams. On other occasions, the instructor develops a better understanding of why the student might need to ask many clarifying questions during the exam.

Besides performance-based strategies, the LDS staff help students address questions about **medications**. Some students want to discuss their fears and hopes about medications as they decide whether or not to try this treatment approach. Other students want to find a more effective medication than the one they currently use. LDS staff members always encourage students to work carefully with their physicians about these concerns.

Some students need help in organizing what they want to tell or ask their doctors. Staff members help students identify physicians specializing in treating adults; share literature on AD/HD medications; and, help students record patterns in their response to medications. LD specialists have helped some students create individual titration logs to document these patterns. These logs facilitate a student's discussion with his/her physician.

Another service now offered helps students develop strategies for managing their medication compliance. Initially, LDS staff didn't understand how difficult it is for someone with AD/HD to take a pill two or three times a day. This process becomes more complicated when physicians give students latitude in their daily regimen. For example, students who begin their Tuesday and Thursday classes at noon may only take two doses on those days, but on Mondays, Wednesdays and Fridays take three doses when their first class is at 8 a.m. Other students take "drug holidays" on weekends or when they go out to socialize at night. Again, this is often done with their physician's consent. The LD specialists do not question the appropriateness of these intermittent schedules, but they do see how difficult it can be for some students to follow them. These varying patterns magnify the problem of habit formation in students who lack internal regulation and self-monitoring skills.

Coaching is now being offered to students with AD/HD. Students' feedback emphasized the benefits of adding coaching to the range of strategies offered at LDS. The following section will identify concerns about coaching that staff members addressed as a team, then identify the coaching services now offered by the LDS staff.

LD specialists at LDS had a number of concerns about coaching:

- **Promoting independence** – The staff was concerned that private coaches would not help their clients develop independent skills. LDS staff were hesitant to offer coaching if it failed to help students internalize performance skills they could eventually use on their own.

- **Screening** – LDS staff members understood coaches' desire to separate their work from that of therapists and to delay work with a client until he/she had addressed ongoing psychological issues. But, they did not anticipate being able to withhold coaching when students requested this service at LDS. They realized that it would be very helpful to clarify students' affective needs when they began working at LDS. The staff also knew the importance of clarifying the extent of their coaching expertise and developing an active referral network to help students who needed to look at affective issues.

- **Logistics** – LDS staff members heard of coaches "making house calls", and conducting phone sessions in the evenings and on weekends. They didn't want to offer a service requiring extended hours, nor were they comfortable working with students in their homes/rooms.

- **Scope** – Coaches work with clients on a range of needs including life skills such as completing tax forms and finding new jobs. Given the mission of LDS and the staff members' expertise in academic interventions, the staff decided to maintain a focus on students' course-related needs.

- **Administrative support** – A fundamental concern that staff members needed to look into was that of administrative support. They wondered if administrators and faculty would share their understanding of the impact of AD/HD so that the need for new services for this population would seem reasonable.

After much planning and discussion, LDS staff members now offer a range of coaching services that have been adapted from private practice. LD specialists take great care when talking with current or prospective students, in distinguishing between private ADD coaching and the services they offer. An on-going dialogue with students about these services and the extent to which they meet students' needs continue. In addition, LDS staff continue consultation with colleagues on and off campus to learn more about this topic and its implications for their program model.

With these caveats in mind, the following section will summarize the coaching principles and techniques that have been added to the services offered to students at LDS.

- **A belief about students:** LD specialists first recognized that many students with AD/HD do, indeed, have effective answers to their academic problems. This concept, basic as it may seem, has fundamentally altered many of their interactions with these students. It also changed how they view and define their role while coaching. In many ways, this shift feels similar to the change in roles classroom teachers experienced in the 1980's, when they began using personal computers as instructional tools. They found themselves transitioning from a highly didactic role to that of a facilitator as they encouraged students to pursue their own learning goals. LDS staff members are continuing to learn effective ways to "shift gears" with students when their needs change from coaching to strategies work. When teaching strategies, staff members are still fairly didactic as they present and model new skills.

- **Designing the alliance:** LDS staff members have adapted a decision-making technique from private coaches known as "designing the alliance." Designing the alliance is the process of working with each student to develop mutually agreed on ground rules for interaction. LD specialists define their role as coaches at this point and help students define their needs. They ask students about their communication styles and preferences to learn how to provide direct, honest feedback in a comfortable manner. They specifically ask how they might redirect students or otherwise respond if the student's AD/HD characteristics begin to limit their progress toward their own goals. Coaches refer to this as "holding the person's agenda."

Prior consensus about the type of feedback that a student would want in these situations, helps staff members offer structure without being controlling or judgmental. They have learned to design the alliance with students from the first time they meet with them each semester. Otherwise, it can be counter productive to try to ease into this later when problems occur. These questions invite the student to "engineer" his/her environment to be in control of the learning process. This type of interaction establishes from the outset that the student is a capable and independent learner. Some questions that staff members might ask students when designing the alliance include:

(1) If I observe that you have lost track of what you were talking about, would you like me to give you any feedback? If so, what could I say or do that would be helpful?
(2) Would it be helpful to you to get back in touch with me to report on your progress toward a goal you've set in our session? If so, how would you like to do this? Would you like to e-mail me or leave a voicemail message, or would another approach work better?
(3) Having identified a short-term goal that you want to work on with me, how frequently would you like to meet to accomplish this goal? How long should our sessions be in order to be productive for you?

➢ **Communication skills:** Once ground rules have been established, a number of techniques are used to help students clarify their problems and develop effective solutions. At this stage, coaching involves asking students succinct questions to help them stop and reflect. LDS staff members have learned to limit what they tell students and, instead, pose a question that prompts them to verbalize (or write, or diagram, or e-mail to themselves...) the directions or reminders they will need later to carry out a task.

Two specific coaching techniques that can accomplish this goal include "holding up the mirror" and using the "ant/eagle view." When they hold up the mirror, they remind students of their past successes as well as their past difficulties. This helps students refocus on what they can do to accomplish their goal. The ant/eagle view is a reframing technique that helps students consciously shift their focus between the "big picture" and details of a current project. This technique helps students remind themselves of their overall goals as well as the steps they need to take to reach those goals.

➢ **Problem-solving:** Coaching techniques, such as those previously described allow LDS staff to model, in an overt fashion, effective problem-solving techniques. **They have concluded that problem-solving is the overarching strategy so lacking in many college students with AD/HD.** To problem solve, one needs to stop and reflect; to clarify what the problem is; to draw upon past experiences for insights; and to look ahead in time to anticipate barriers and to feel hope about reaching one's goals. The LD specialists' understanding of the need to teach this skill to students with AD/HD has grown in equal measure to their understanding of the disability and its impact.

➢ **Evaluating the effectiveness of coaching.** LDS staff continue to monitor the effectiveness of coaching. Coaching works when students get their work done and learn more about regulating their own behavior in the process. When repeated coaching fails to help students accomplish these goals, LDS staff members have learned new ways to address this pattern openly and honestly with students.

At times, this pattern results when students are not successfully addressing affective issues. Students with untreated anxiety or depression for example, can find it extremely difficult to change their behavior or to follow through on decisions. Other students may not be ready for coaching, despite having expressed an interest in this service. Being coached entails being accountable to someone else for following through on one's plans and decisions. Not all students are comfortable with this type of relationship. Of course, a lack of progress in a coaching relationship may mean that the coach needs to strengthen his/her skills, or that the coach and the student need to redesign their alliance in order to make changes in how the coaching services are being offered.

The importance of learning how to "get things done" cannot be overlooked when considering the self-esteem of college students with AD/HD. Too many of these students live in shame due to repeated histories of disappointing themselves and others. They know *what* they need to be doing; they are less sure about *how* they will get it done or even ***if*** they can get it done.

Therefore, they agonize over ***why*** they encounter such difficulties despite their intelligence and achievements in other areas. Coaching is effective because it helps college students with AD/HD reframe their understanding of themselves as capable, competent individuals who can count on themselves and can be counted on by others.

In addition to individualized services, LDS offers **group activities** designed to respond to the needs of students with AD/HD. The staff has hosted several seminars to provide current information about diagnosis and treatment issues. Local professionals expert in this area have been invited to discuss current trends. Student volunteers have helped the staff plan and conduct these events. At one, students shared examples of effective time management strategies. In addition, staff members have met with groups of students who watched and discussed a wonderful video, *ADD: The Race Inside My Head* (George Washington University, 1996).

These activities address a number of expressed needs of students with AD/HD. First, they are time efficient; students can come to an event and, two hours later, leave with useful insights and encouragement. Second, they enhance disability awareness in a group of students who often have recent diagnoses and, therefore, many questions about the disability. Third, group events build community. Many students with AD/HD feel alone in their experiences and welcome the opportunity to learn that they are not so isolated after all. This desire to network with peers is shared by students with LD, but the newness of the need for accommodations and services in college that many students with AD/HD confront makes this issue particularly poignant.

CONCLUSION

The authors have argued that college students with AD/HD are different from students with LD in a number of ways. Despite these differences, students with AD/HD benefit from services and seek them out in equal numbers to students with LD on the UNC-CH campus. Over the past three years, the LDS office has found it necessary to adapt some of these services to better meet the needs of students with AD/HD. They believe that offering services to students with this disability embraces the spirit of the law in the same way that offering services to students with LD does.

Both types of students have the intellectual potential to learn new ways to minimize the impact of their disability. Students with LD and AD/HD encounter the impact of their respective disabilities in situations where accommodations may not be feasible. Students with AD/HD, for example, can find it difficult to stay focused during a long conversation. How does one accommodate for such demands, particularly when medications are not effective?

Despite the changes made to their program model, the staff at LDS still has a great deal to learn. They will continue to collect data and to engage in professional training. Both of these activities will help them refine their understanding of students' needs and strengthen their ability to respond effectively. Communicating openly with administrators and faculty members as they all learn more about the impact of AD/HD in adults will continue. Ongoing dialogue is important as a proactive response to the doubts and concerns some university members have about the legitimacy of an AD/HD diagnosis and students' needs for accommodations and services.

The authors recognize that college students with AD/HD, like their counterparts with LD are a heterogeneous group with countless individual differences. Despite these differences, they share many wonderful strengths. Offering services to these students provides them with a way to develop their strengths for greater independence and success, both in school and in life. Teaching strategies and offering coaching services lead to moments of frustration as well as joy. Students with AD/HD can bring high levels of energy and enthusiasm to their sessions. They are creative and curious about the world. When they focus their intelligence on areas of interest, they often develop unique insights that add richness to the world of academic discourse.

Despite their characteristic difficulties with getting things done, these students possess a tenacity that drives them to their goals despite many bumps along the way. They have been among the most helpful teachers of LDS staff during its learning curve about AD/HD. Other service providers who would like to learn more about effective programming for students with this disability are encouraged to seek out the experts in their offices.

References

American Psychiatric Disorder. (1994). *Diagnostic and statistical manual of mental disorders (4th ed.).* Washington, DC: Author.

Anderson, P.L. (1998, Winter). Essential support services for postsecondary students with learning disabilities: Highlights from a delphi study. *Postsecondary Disability Network News, (32),* 1-6.

Barkley, R.A. (1997, August). Update on a theory of AD/HD and its clinical implications. *The AD/HD Report, 5,* 10-16.

Brinckerhoff, L.C., Shaw, S.F., & McGuire, J.M. (1993). *Promoting post secondary education for students with learning disabilities.* Austin, TX: PRO-ED, Inc. (see pp. 251-253).

Byron, J. and Parker, D.R. (1997, Spring). Get on the bus: Responding to the needs of college students with AD/HD. *Postsecondary Disability Net work News, (30),* 1-5.

Crux, S.C. (1991). *Learning strategies for adults: Compensations for learning disabilities.* Toronto, Ontario: Wall & Emerson, Inc.,(pp. 13-16).

Mangrum, C.T. and Strichart, S.S. (1997). *Colleges with programs for students with learning disabilities or attention deficit disorders.* Princeton, NJ: Petersons.

Nadeau, K.G. (1995 Spring/Fall). An introduction to the special issue on attention deficit disorder. *Journal of Postsecondary Education and Disability, 11,* 1-2.

Price, L. (1993). Psychosocial characteristics and issues of adults with learning disabilities. In Brinckerhoff, L.C., Shaw, S.F., & McGuire, J.M. (Eds.), *Promoting postsecondary education for students with learning disabilities.* (pp. 137-168). Austin, TX: PRO-ED, Inc.

Resources

ADDA (National Attention Deficit Disorder Association); 9930 Johnnycake Ridge,Suite 3E, Mentor, OH 44060; (216) 350-9595.

Adults with Attention Deficit Disorders Listserv; send subscription request to **ADDULT@SJUVM.STJOHNS.EDU**

American Coaching Association. Susan Sussman, Founder; (610) 825-4505.

George Washington University (Producer). (1996). ADD: The race inside my head [Videotape]. To order, contact AHEAD, P.O. Box 21192, Columbus, OH 43221-0192; (614) 488-1174.

Inspiration Software, Inc., 7412 SW Beaverton, Hillsdale Hwy, Suite 102, Portland, OR 97225-2167; (503) 297-3004. □

GUIDELINES FOR DOCUMENTATION OF ATTENTION DEFICIT/ HYPERACTIVITY DISORDER IN ADOLESCENTS AND ADULTS

Developed by The Consortium on AD/HD Documentation
Loring Brinckerhoff, Ph.D., Chairman

In the fall of 1997, seven members of the Association on Higher Education and Disability (AHEAD) met at Dartmouth College to develop a set of guidelines for documenting AD/HD that would closely parallel the *AHEAD Guidelines for Documentation of a Learning Disability in Adolescents and Adults* (AHEAD, 1997). The members of the Consortium were intent on developing standard criteria for documenting AD/HD that could be used by disability service providers, licensing and testing agencies, and consumers. The final draft of the guidelines was sent out for further review to some of the leading physicians, neuropsychologists, postsecondary service providers and university scholars in the field of AD/HD. The Consortium acknowledges these professionals for their thoughtful feedback in the refinement of the final product which is presented here.

INTRODUCTION

The primary purpose of these guidelines is to educate our colleagues and consumers as to how to determine whether the AD/HD documentation submitted is sufficient to support the disability claim and the accommodation(s) being requested. Criteria that are addressed in the Consortium's AD/HD guidelines include: qualifications of the evaluator; recency of the documentation; comprehensive documentation components including evidence of early and current impairment; relevant testing; identification criteria from the *Diagnostic and Statistical Manual of Mental Disorders - Fourth Edition* (DSM-IV) (American Psychiatric Association, 1994); a specific diagnosis and interpretive summary; and a rationale for the recommended accommodation(s).

An additional intent of the guidelines is to provide "a springboard" for the development of policies that could be tailored to the unique needs of a given setting, state, or region. The guidelines are not designed to be a "boilerplate". Practitioners are encouraged to tailor these guidelines to suit the needs of their respective settings.

As one service provider recently commented, disability service providers should no longer be placed in a position of having to accept " incredibly insufficient little notes on a prescription pad" as documentation for an attention deficit disorder. Although the Consortium guidelines may best be viewed as a "work in progress" it is hoped that they will provide our field with additional guidance and an acceptable standard so that misconceptions regarding the documentation of ADHD in adolescents and adults can be minimized and opportunities for a productive dialogue, on a case-by-case basis, can be facilitated.

GUIDELINES FOR DOCUMENTATION OF AD/HD IN ADOLESCENTS AND ADULTS

Introduction

The Consortium's mission is to develop standard criteria for documenting attention deficit disorders, with and without hyperactivity (AD/HD). These guidelines can be used by postsecondary personnel, examining, certifying, and licensing agencies, and consumers who require documentation to determine reasonable and appropriate accommodation(s) for individuals with AD/HD. Although the more generic term, Attention Deficit Disorder (ADD), is frequently used, the official nomenclature in the Diagnostic and Statistical manual of Mental Disorders (4th ed.) (DSM-IV) (American Psychiatric Association, 1994) is Attention Deficit/Hyperactivity Disorder (AD/HD) which is used in these guidelines. The guidelines provide consumers, professional diagnosticians, and service providers with a common understanding and knowledge base of the components of documentation which are necessary to validate the existence of AD/HD, its impact on the individual's educational performance, and the need for accommodation(s). The information and documentation to be submitted should be comprehensive in order to avoid or reduce unnecessary time delays in decision-making related to the provision of services. In the main section of the document, the Consortium presents guidelines in four important areas: 1) qualifications of the evaluator; 2) recency of documentation; 3) comprehensiveness of the documentation to substantiate the AD/HD; and 4) evidence to establish a rationale to support the need for accommoda-tion(s). *Attached to these guidelines are the diagnostic criteria for AD/HD from the Diagnostic and Statistical Manual of Mental Disorders (4th ed.) (DSM-IV) (American Psychiatric Association, 1994) which are presented in this work in the Appendix.

Under the Americans with Disabilities Act (ADA) and Section 504 of the Rehabilitation Act of 1973, individuals with disabilities are protected from discrimination and assured services. In order to establish that an individual is covered under ADA, the documentation must indicate that the disability substantially limits some major life activity, including learning. The following documentation guidelines are provided in the interest of assuring that documentation of AD/HD demonstrates an impact on a major life activity and supports the request for accommodations, academic adjustments and/or auxiliary aids.

DOCUMENTATION

I. A Qualifies Professional Must Conduct the Evaluation

Professionals conducting assessments and rendering diagnoses of AD/HD must have training in differential diagnosis of AD/HD and the full range of psychiatric disorders. The name, title, and professional credentials of the evaluator, including information about license or certification as well as the area of specialization, employment, and state or province in which the individual practices should be clearly stated in the documentation. The following professionals would generally be considered qualified to evaluate and diagnose AD/HD provided they have comprehensive training in the differential diagnosis of AD/HD and direct experience with an adolescent or adult AD/HD population:clinical psychologists, neuropsychologists, psychiatrists, and other relevantly trained medical doctors. It may be appropriate to use a clinical team approach consisting of a variety of educational, medical, and counseling professionals with training in the evaluation of AD/HD in adolescents and adults.

Use of diagnostic terminology indicating and AD/HD by someone whose training and experience are not in these fields is not acceptable. It is also not appropriate for professionals to evaluate members of their own families. All reports should be on letterhead, typed, dated, signed, and otherwise legible. The receiving institution or agency has the responsibility to maintain the confidentiality of the individual's records.

II. Documentation Should Be Current

Because the provision of all reasonable accommodations and services are based upon assessment of the current impact of the disability on academic performance, it is in an individuals's best interest to provide recent and appropriate documentation. In most cases, this means that a diagnostic evaluation has been completed within the last three years. Flexibility in accepting documentation under certain conditions if the previous assessment is applicable to the current or anticipated setting, If documentation us inadequate in scope or content, or does not address the individuals's current level of functioning and need for accommodation(s), reevaluation may be warranted. Furthermore, observed changes may have occurred in the individual's performance since previous assessment, or new medication(s) may have been prescribed or discontinued since the previous assessment was conducted. In such cases, it may be necessary to update the evaluation report. The update should include a detailed assessment of the current impact of the AD/HD and interpretive summary of relevant information (see Section III, G) and the previous diagnostic report.

III. Documentation Should Be Comprehensive

A. Evidence of Early Impairment

Because AD/HD is, by definition, first exhibited in childhood (although it may not have been formally diagnosed) and manifests itself in more than one setting, relevant historical information is essential. The following should be included in a comprehensive assessment: clinical summary of objective, historical information establishing symptomatology indicative of AD/HD throughout childhood, adolescence, and adulthood as garnered from transcripts, report cards, teacher comments, tutoring evaluations, past psychological testing, and third party interviews when available.

B. Evidence of Current Impairment

In addition to providing evidence of a childhood history of an impairment, the following areas must be investigated:

1. Statement of Presenting Problem

A history of the individual's presenting attentional symptoms should be provided, including evidence of ongoing impulsive/ hyperactive or inattentive behaviors that significantly impair functioning in two or more settings.

2. Diagnostic Interview

The information collected for the summary of the diagnostic interview should consist of more than self-report, as information from third party sources is critical in the diagnosis of AD/HD. The diagnostic interview with information from a variety of sources should include, but not necessarily be limited to, the following: history of presenting attentional symptoms, including evidence of ongoing impulsive/hyperactive or inattentive behavior that has significantly impaired functioning over time; developmental history; family history for presence of AD/HD and other educational, learning, physical or psychological difficulties deemed relevant by the examiner; relevant medical and medication history, including the absence of a medical basis for the symptoms being evaluated; relevant psychosocial history and any relevant interventions; a thorough academic history of elementary, secondary, and postsecondary education; review of prior psychoeducational test reports to determine whether a pattern of strengths or weaknesses is supportive of attention or learning problems; relevant employment history; description of current functional limitations pertaining to an educational setting that are presumably a direct result of problems with attention; and relevant history of prior therapy.

C. Rule Out of Alternative Diagnoses or Explanations

The evaluator must investigate and discuss the possibility of dual diagnoses, and alternative or coexisting mood, behavioral, neurological, and/or personality disorders which may confound the diagnosis of AD/HD. This process should include exploration of possible, alternative diagnoses, and medical and psychiatric disorders as well as educational and cultural factors impacting the individual which may result in behaviors mimicking an Attention Deficit/ Hyperactivity Disorder.

D. Relevant Testing

Neuropsychological or psychoeducational assessment is important in determining the currant impact of the disorder on the individual's ability to function in academically related settings. The evaluator should objectively review and include with the evaluation report relevant background information to support the diagnosis. If grade equivalents are reported, they must be accompanied by standard scores and/or percentiles. Test scores or subtest scores alone should not be used as the sole measure for the diagnostic decision regarding AD/HD. Selected subtest scores from measures of intellectual ability, memory functions tests, attention or tracking tests, or continuous performance tests do not in and of themselves establish the presence or absence of AD/HD. Checklists and/or surveys can serve to supplement the diagnostic profile but in and of themselves are not adequate for the diagnosis of AD/HD and do not substitute foe clinical observations and sound diagnostic judgement. All data must logically reflect a substantial limitation to learning for which the individual is requesting the accommodation.

E. Identification of DSM-IV Criteria

According to DSM-IV. "the essential feature of AD/HD is a persistent pattern of inattention and/or hyperactivity-impulsivity that is more frequent and severe than is frequently observed in individuals at a comparable level of development" (p.78). A diagnostic report should include a review and discussion of the DSM-IV criteria for AD/HD both currently and retrospectively and specify which symptoms are present (See Appendix A for DSM-IV criteria).

In diagnosing AD/HD, it is particularly important to address the following criteria: symptoms of hyperactivity/impulsivity or inattention that cause impairment which must have been present for at least the past six months; impairment from the symptoms present in two or more settings (for example, school, work, and home); clear evidence of significant impairment in social, academic, or occupational functioning; and symptoms which do not occur exclusively during the course of a Pervasive Developmental Disorder, Schizophrenia, or other Psychotic Disorder and are not better accounted for by another mental disorder (e.g. Mood Disorder, Anxiety Disorder, Dissociative Disorder, or a Personality Disorder).

F. Documentation Must Include a Specific Diagnosis

The report must include a specific diagnosis of AD/HD based on the DSM-IV diagnostic criteria. The diagnostician should use direct language in the diagnosis of AD/HD, avoiding the use of terms such as "suggests," is indicative of," or "attention Problems."

Individuals who report only problems with organization, test anxiety, memory and concentration in selective situations do not fit the proscribed diagnostic criteria for AD/HD. Given that many individuals benefit from prescribed medications and therapies, a positive response to medication by itself does not confirm a diagnosis, nor does the use of medication in and of itself support or negate the need for accommodation(s).

G. An Interpretative Summary Should be Provided

A well-written interpretative summary based on a comprehensive evaluation process is a necessary component of the documentation. Because AD/HD is in many ways a diagnosis which is based upon the interpretation of historical data and observation, as well as other diagnostic information, it is essential that professional judgement be utilized in the development of a summary, which should include:

1. demonstration of the evaluator's having ruled out alternative explanations for inattentiveness, impulsivity, and/or hyperactivity as a result of psychological or medical disorders or non-cognitive factors;
2. indication of how patterns of inattentiveness, impulsivity, and/or hyperactivity across the life span and across settings are used to determine the presence of AD/HD;
3. indication of whether or not the student was evaluated while on medication, and whether or not there is a positive response to the prescribed treatment;
4. indication and discussion of the substantial limitation to learning presented by the AD/HD and the degree to which it impacts the individual in the learning context for which accommodations are being requested; and
5. indication as to why specific accommodations are needed and how the effects of AD/HD symptoms, as designated by the DSM-IV, are mediated by the accommodation(s).

IV. Each Accommodation Recommended by the Evaluator Should Include a Rationale

The evaluator(s) should describe the impact, if any, of the diagnosed AD/HD on a specific major life activity as well as the degree of impact on the individual. The diagnostic report should include specifics recommendations for accommodations that are realistic and that postsecondary institutions examining, certifying, and licensing agencies can reasonably provide. A detailed explanation should be provided as to why each accommodation is recommended and should be correlated with specific functional limitations determined through interview, observation, and/or testing. Although prior documentation may have been useful in determining appropriate services in the past, current documentation should validate the need for services based on the individuals's present level of functioning in the educational setting. A school plan such as an Individual Education Program (IEP) or a 504 plan is insufficient documentation in and of itself but can be included as part of a more comprehensive evaluation report. The documentation should include any record or prior accommodation or auxiliary aids, including information about specific conditions under which accommodations were used (e.g., standardized testing, final exams, licensing or certification examinations) and whether or not they benefitted the individual. However, a prior history of accommodations, without demonstration of a current need, does not in itself warrant the provision of a like accommodation. If no prior accommodations were provided, the qualified professional and/or the individual should include a detailed explanation as to why no accommodations were used in the past and why accommodations are needed at this time.

Because of the challenge of distinguishing normal behaviors and developmental patterns of adolescents and adults (e.g., procrastination, restlessness, boredom, academic underachievement or failure, low self-esteem, and chronic tardiness or in attendance) from clinically significant impairment, a multifaceted evaluation should address the intensity and frequency of the symptoms and whether these behaviors constitute an impairment in a major life activity.

Reasonable accommodation(s) may help to ameliorate the disability and to minimize its impact on the student's attention, impulsivity, and distractibility. The determination for reasonable accommodation(s) rests with the designated disability contact person working in collaboration with the individual with the disability and when appropriate, college faculty. The receiving institution or agency has a responsibility to maintain confidentiality of the evaluation and may not release any part of the documentation without the individual's informed consent.

References

American Psychiatric Association. (1994) *Diagnostic and statistical manual of mental disorders (4th ed.).* Washington, DC: Author.

□

Consortium on AD/HD Documentation

Loring C. Brinckerhoff, Chairperson,
Educational Testing Service

Kim M. Dempsey,
Law School Admission Council

Cyndi Jordan,
University of Tennessee - Memphis

Shelby R. Keiser,
National Board of Medical Examiners

Joan M. McGuire,
University of Connecticut- Storrs

Nancy W. Pompain,
Dartmouth College

Louise H. Russell,
Harvard University

THE VALIDITY OF RATING SCALES USED TO ASSESS AD/HD IN COLLEGE STUDENTS

Julie M. Sayer, B.A., and Stuart A. Vyse, Ph.D.
Department of Psychology
Connecticut College

This study evaluated the discriminant validity of three current measures used for diagnosis of Attention Deficit Hyperactivity Disorder (AD/HD) in adults: The Brown ADD Scale (Brown, 1996); The College Level AD/HD Questionnaire (Nadeau, 1994); and the College Situations Questionnaire (CSQ). Seventy-eight college students and four non-college students participated in the study. Seventeen of the eighty-two participants were diagnosed with AD/HD. Significant differences in mean scores were found among the college students with AD/HD, and the adult AD/HD group on all three measures.

INTRODUCTION

Attention Deficit Hyperactivity Disorder (AD/HD) is one of the most widely researched childhood disorders today. Although the majority of research has focused on children with the disorder, current research suggests that the disorder can continue into adolescence and adulthood (Barkley, 1990; Gittleman, Mannuzza, Shenker, & Bongura, 1985). More recently, the *Diagnostic and Statistical Manual of Mental Disorders* (American Psychiatric Association, 1994) recognizes the continuation of AD/HD symptoms into adolescence and adulthood. Yet, much remains unknown about the manifestation of the disorder in adolescents and adults.

Attention Deficit Hyperactivity Disorder in children is defined by the three primary symptoms of hyperactivity, inattention, and impulsivity. Current research suggests that these three symptoms may not always be the primary symptoms of the disorder in adults (Brown, 1995).

ASSESSMENT OF AD/HD IN ADULTS

The *DSM-IV* (American Psychiatric Association, 1994) does not differentiate between the AD/HD diagnostic criteria for adults and children. Mental health professionals in clinical practice are finding that the three primary tiers of the disorder (attention, impulsivity, and hyperactivity) may not carry over into adult symptomatology. Many adults with AD/HD do not display overt hyperactive symptoms. Adults are more likely to appear fidgety rather than display gross motor hyperactivity. It is likely that they have learned to control the hyperactivity or it has lessened as they have matured. A broader perspective of the disorder focuses not only on attention, hyperactivity, and impulsivity, but on organization, concentration, mood lability, time management, and chronic underachievement (Brown, 1995).

Since there are few empirically validated measures to clinically assess AD/HD in adults, the core symptoms of the disorder in adults remain elusive. Leimkuhler (1994) describes the disorder as an inconsistency of directed attention. The individual may be unable to sustain attention on important aspects and may instead focus on external stimuli or minor details. It is suggested that this indicates why individuals with AD/HD are frequently distracted and pay attention to irrelevant details. Ratey (1995) suggested that the disorder has a major impact on interpersonal relationships and emotional functioning, which may be often overlooked as symptoms of a disorder.

Currently, there are no specific diagnostic criteria to assess AD/HD in adults. Mental health professionals have adapted scales from childhood AD/HD measurements. Many measures created for diagnosing the disorder in children focus on parent and teacher rating scales. The Utah criteria proposed by Wender (1985) is a widely used diagnostic tool for recognizing AD/HD in adults. A parent or sibling may report on the adult's previous childhood behaviors. The Utah criteria are based on childhood behaviors of the adult, and, the measure emphasizes continued hyperactive symptomatology. The scale does not address current behaviors of the adult. Conceptualization of the disorder in adulthood is based solely on the presence of AD/HD in childhood. However, many individuals display AD/HD symptoms even though they may not have had overt AD/HD symptoms in childhood (Biggs, 1995).

Since the Utah Rating Scale emphasizes hyperactivity, it can overlook non-hyperactive adults with AD/HD. Hyperactivity, although a major symptom in diagnosing the disorder in children, is not always apparent in diagnosing adults. As Brown (1995) discusses, the Utah criteria only focus on one of the most severe forms of the disorder, and overlook the predominantly inattentive forms of the disorder described in the *DSM-IV* (American Psychiatric Association, 1994). Identifying the individual with the predominantly inattentive type AD/HD, may be elusive (Tzelepis, Schubiner, & Warbasse, 1995). These individuals may not have had behavior problems as children, and may have functioned well academically, causing them to be overlooked. Since a broader perspective is necessary for diagnosing the disorder in adults, a scale that only focuses on childhood behaviors is not adequate.

Recently two assessment instruments have been published for diagnosis of AD/HD in adults (Brown, 1996; Nadeau, 1994). Both scales emphasize the broader perspective of the disorder. The measures deal with organization, time management, mood lability, interpersonal and social skills, forgetfulness, concentration, and chronic underachievement. The scales are relatively new and it is not known how widely they're used in clinical practice.

Brown (1996) has developed two scales to measure ADD in adolescents and adults. Development of the scales was based on his clinical experience with students who suffered from problems of chronic underachievement, yet possessed high IQ scores. Brown (1995) has found that although the students met the *DSM*-criteria for attention deficits, they did not display symptoms of hyperactivity and impulsivity. Brown (1996) states, "The Scales comprise a description of interrelated cognitive and affective symptoms often reported by persons diagnosed with Attention-Deficit Disorders" (p. 5). Brown (1996) suggests that the disorder has a cognitive and affective basis which indicates that the diagnostic criteria proposed for AD/HD may be too narrow and too focused on the three primary tiers of inattention, hyperactivity, and impulsivity, rather than recognizing additional symptoms displayed by adults with the disorder.

Brown (1996) organizes the ADD Scales into five categories. The first category, organizing and activating to work, is concerned with symptoms such as difficulty getting started on desk work and daily routines, problems waking up, and organizing tasks. The second category describes difficulties sustaining attention and concentration during work-related tasks, and reading. Sustaining energy and effort throughout the day is the third category. The fourth category, managing affective interference, centers mainly around mood lability. The last category Brown describes as utilizing working memory and accessing recall. This category describes symptoms such as forgetfulness, and difficulty in recall and other memory tasks.

Brown (1996) proposes that the scales be used for initial screening of Attention Deficit Disorders. He suggests that a further, more in-depth evaluation take place before the actual diagnosis is made. A number of other screening devices are used including semi-structured interviews and attention level screening devices.

Nadeau (1994) has developed a scale that measures 19 different categories. Her scale has not been tested for validity and is based on her clinical experience. She suggests that the scale be used as a structural assessment interview (Biggs, 1995), and has recently revised it to be used as a screening device for assessing college students with attentional difficulties.

Biggs (1995) states that the measures designed by Nadeau for both adolescent and college students differ from other screening devices because the scales cover a broader range of issues that the clinician would need during the course of treatment, rather than simply focusing on the AD/HD triad of distractibility, impulsivity, and hyperactivity (p. 112). Nadeau (1994) includes categories such as self-discipline, time management, frustration tolerance, sleep patterns, self-esteem, and social/interpersonal. She evaluates the disorder in terms of difficulties unique to adulthood. Some of these difficulties may be apparent in children but are unlikely to become problems until the individual is functioning independently.

Currently, the most reliable criterion for assessing AD/HD in adults is a semi-structured interview. Both Brown (1996) and Barkley (1991) have created interview criteria. Since adults display differing symptoms and problems, the semi-structured interview can pinpoint major problems or symptoms the client may have. The semi-structured interview deals with questions about the adult's family life, substance abuse, childhood problems, and attention difficulties.

Additional measures are often used when making an adequate diagnosis of AD/HD. The Wechsler Adult Intelligence Scale-Revised (WAIS-R) identifies verbal or spatial/visual tasks with which the client may have difficulty (Biggs, 1995). The WAIS-R scores can be compared to academic performance to rule out the possibility of "lack of ability" in the individual. The Continuous Performance Test (CPT, 2.0) can be used to provide information about attention levels. The CPT developed by Keith Conners (1985) is a computer program that measures visual attention levels during a specific task, such as recognizing particular letters.

Another continuous performance test used is the TOVA (Greenberg, 1993). Other scales measure divided and alternative attention. Sohlberg and Mateer (1987) have designed a card-sorting task to measure this aspect of attention. Tests that measure memory, impulsivity, problem-solving, and cognitive processing may also be useful for diagnosing adults with AD/HD. Biggs (1995) describes many of these scales in detail discussing their ability to discriminate between individuals with and without AD/HD.

SCALES TO DIAGNOSE AD/HD

The present study evaluated the discriminative validity of three current measures used to diagnose AD/HD in adults, primarily college students: the Brown ADD Scale (Brown, 1996); the College Level AD/HD Questionnaire (Nadeau, 1994); and the College Situation Questionnaire (CSQ). It was hypothesized that college students with AD/HD would have significantly higher mean scores on all three of the measures indicating more severe and persistent symptoms of AD/HD compared to controls.

The normative results of the scales indicated the symptoms which were more problematic for the college students with AD/HD compared to the control groups. Reliability scores were collected on the Nadeau College Level Questionnaire (1994) and the College Situations Questionnaire. It was hypothesized that the scales would have strong reliability scores.

DuPaul (1990) has developed two scales, the Home Situations Questionnaire-Revised (HSQ-R), and the School Situations Questionnaire-Revised (SSQ-R). The measures focus on levels of attention and concentration children display in the home and at school. The questions from these measures were adapted by the researcher to focus specifically on college academic and nonacademic situations. The measure was titled the College Situations Questionnaire (CSQ). The validity of this adapted measure was evaluated in the study.

It was hypothesized that college students with AD/HD would report more severe levels of inattention in both academic and non-academic situations. Seventy-eight college students and four non-college students participated in the study. Seventeen of the eighty-two participants were diagnosed with AD/HD. The participants in the study were divided into four groups. Two groups included individuals diagnosed with AD/HD and the other two groups were control subjects.

- The first group of participants consisted of 13 college students diagnosed with AD/HD (7 females, and 6 males). To be included in the sample, students had to have written confirmation of the diagnosis of AD/HD from a physician, psychologist or psychiatrist. The mean age was 21.5 years.

- The second group of participants included 4 female members of CH.A.D.D. (Children and Adults with Attention Deficit Disorder) support group from Waterford, Ct. Each participant indicated that he/she was clinically diagnosed with AD/HD. Participants ranged in age from 20-45 years; the mean age was 33.8 years.

- The third group of participants included 21 Introductory Psychology 101 and 102 students (15 females, and 6 males) who participated as the first control group for course credit. The participants ranged in age from 18-21 years; the mean age was 19.9 years.

- The fourth group of participants was randomly solicited from the college library as the second control group. Forty-three students (30 females, 13 males) completed the questionnaires. The age range of the participants was 18-23 yrs; the mean age was 20.2 yrs.

MEASURES

Brown Attention Deficit Disorder Scale (Brown, 1996). The Brown ADD Scale contains 40 questions about feelings or behaviors pertaining to AD/HD symptoms in the last 6 months (Brown, 1996). The scale concentrates on five specific areas: activating and organizing work; sustaining attention and concentration; sustaining energy and effort; managing affective interference; utilizing working memory; and accessing recall. Participants rated the behavior as occurring never, once a week or less, twice a week, or almost daily.

The Nadeau College Level AD/HD Questionnaire (Nadeau, 1994). The Nadeau College Level AD/HD Questionnaire contains 88 questions divided into 14 sections: inattention; impulsivity; hyperactivity; distractibility; hyperfocusing; time management; self-discipline; organization/structure; stimulants; substance abuse; memory; frustration tolerance; anger; and academics. Questions are answered on a five-point Likert scale from, "I feel this statement describes me at all," to "I feel this statement describes me to a large degree."

College Situations Questionnaire (CSQ). The College Situations Questionnaire was adapted by the researcher from the Revised Home and School Situations Questionnaire created by DuPaul (1990). The questions from these measures were adapted specifically for college students, and focused on attention and concentration problems a college student with AD/HD may have in particular academic and nonacademic situations. The measure consisted of 16 questions answered on a 9-point Likert scale from mild to severe. Two items on the measure, "Do you have problems paying attention or concentrating during labs or while playing computer games?, were removed from the questionnaire because they were not answered by enough participants.

Barkley Semi-Structured Interview (Barkley, 1991) The interview was designed by Barkley (1991) and is used at the University of Massachusetts Medical Center for evaluation of adults who are referred to the clinic because of AD/HD symptoms. The interview consists of 93 questions, but for the purpose of the present study, the interview was cut into 49 questions. The questions were divided into general areas concerning current symptoms and behaviors; childhood behaviors; drug and alcohol abuse; and clinical issues such as past psychiatric history; developmental history; medications; and social history.

***DSM-IV* AD/HD Criteria Checklist.** Included in the questionnaire was an evaluation form for the *DSM-IV* AD/HD Diagnostic Criteria adapted by Brown (1996). The participant indicated the symptoms he/she had in the two areas of inattention and hyperactivity/impulsivity. The *DSM-IV* states that to make a diagnosis, six or more of the listed symptoms must have persisted for the past 6 months in either of the two areas, and these symptoms must be maladaptive to the individual's development.

RESULTS AND DISCUSSION

Significant differences in mean scores were found between the college student AD/HD group and the adult AD/HD group compared to control groups on the Brown ADD Scale (Brown, 1996); Nadeau's College Level AD/HD Questionnaire (Nadeau, 1994); and the College Situations Questionnaire (CSQ). The results indicate that when examining college students, Nadeau's scale (1994) and the CSQ have stronger discriminative validity in recognizing AD/HD than does the Brown ADD Scale (Brown, 1996).

Brown ADD Scale

When comparing the mean scores for each group on the five subscales of the Brown ADD Scale, only three of five subscales revealed significant differences among groups. The sustaining attention and concentration subscale, and the managing affective interference subscale, showed differences among adults with AD/HD and both control groups. Only one subscale utilizing working memory and accessing recall, had significantly different mean scores between the college students with AD/HD and the control group of Introductory Psychology students ($p < .01$).

These results suggest that symptoms of college students with AD/HD could be more cognitively based. Items in the utilizing working memory and accessing recall subscale dealt primarily with symptoms such as easily forgetting; losing; keeping track of things; making mistakes in writing; and difficulty memorizing things. It is suggested that symptoms of AD/HD that may have to do with memory may not be as easily controlled with medication as attention levels and impulsivity. Further research should examine the effects on memory of medication for AD/HD.

Nadeau College Level AD/HD Questionnaire

This is the first investigation of the reliability of the Nadeau College Level AD/HD Questionnaire (Nadeau, 1994). In general, the measure had very strong reliability. Twelve of the 14 subscales had acceptable reliabilities. Two subscales that did not have high alpha values were the substance abuse and stimulant subscales. However, the college population on the average uses more substances and stimulants than do other populations and this may have affected the results.

Compared to Brown's scale (Brpwn, 1996), Nadeau's College Level AD/HD Questionnaire (Nadeau, 1994) scale was more successful in discriminating among college students with AD/HD and control groups. Ten of the 14 subscales showed significant differences among the AD/HD groups and the control groups. Eight of 10 subscales had significantly different mean scores between college students with AD/HD and the control group of Introductory Psychology students. Nadeau's measure had a much broader focus, indicated by 14 subscales, than Brown's measure. Nadeau not only included three tiers of inattention, impulsivity, and hyperactivity; she also included sections about time management, distractibility, hyperfocusing, self-discipline, and organization/structure.

Since her scale revealed the most group differences between individuals with AD/HD compared to both of control groups, it suggests that measurements for diagnosing the disorder offer a variety of symptoms and characteristic behaviors of AD/HD. Nadeau thinks of the disorder not only in terms of central symptoms (inattention, impulsivity, and hyperactivity) but also in the manifestations of these central symptoms (distractibility, hyperfocusing, organization/structure, and academics).

Subscales were significantly different among college students with AD/HD compared to control groups are all related to inattention and impulsivity. Accordingly research on college students with AD/HD, a student with low levels of attention will most likely be easily distracted and will have problems remaining organized (Heiligenstein & Keeling, 1995).

As indicated by previous research, individuals with AD/HD can devote intense levels of attention (hyperfocusing) to something if it interests them, but have more problems sustaining attention if they are not interested in the subject matter (Javorsky, 1994). If an individual has a short attention span and impulsive behaviors, he/she may be easily distracted, and have difficulty organizing his/her life.

College students with AD/HD have been found to have great difficulty with academics (Barkley, 1990). Nadeau's measure indicates significant differences between college students with AD/HD compared to control groups. College students with AD/HD indicated more problems with underachievement, low motivation, and poor grades compared to students without AD/HD.

College students with AD/HD and the adult AD/HD group did not have significantly different mean scores on the substance abuse and stimulants subscales compared to the controls. According to current research findings, college students have higher rates of substance abuse (Javorsky, 1994), but this result was not supported in the study. It is important to note that the measure was self-reported, and individuals may not answer truthfully about the level of substances used. As mentioned earlier, in the college-age population, use of substances is quite common compared to other age groups.

As results of Nadeau's scale suggest, adults with AD/HD may have a wide range of symptoms. As individuals age, they have increased independence and responsibilities. Perhaps the central symptoms of the disorder in children: inattention, impulsivity, and hyperactivitiy, manifest themselves differently in adults with AD/HD. Hyperactivity may wane, and adults may learn how to control short attention spans, yet levels of concentration needed to maintain attention may take up much more energy and lead to other difficulties, such as remembering important things, staying on task, and remaining organized.

College Situations Questionnaire (CSQ)

The College Situations Questionnaire (CSQ) was a new measure used for the first time in this study. The CSQ found significant differences in mean scores between the college students with AD/HD and the control group of Introductory Psychology students. The scale measured levels of attention in specific academic situations like during classes, reading and studying, and academics, etc. The scale was divided into two separate factors.

The only significant differences between the groups occurred with the factor dealing with questions about academic situations. The second factor included questions about situations that were nonacademic in nature and was not significantly different among groups. These results indicate that, like the results from Brown's scale, symptoms of AD/HD in college students may be cognitively based. High levels of inattention and impulsivity may cause individuals to have problems in academic settings. This finding parallels the childhood version of AD/HD especially. The disorder usually comes to the attention of professionals when children begin school. The CSQ can pinpoint specific academic situations where it is the most difficult to pay attention.

This may be helpful in developing coping strategies for the individual by focusing on areas that cause the most problems.

A factor analysis performed on the measure indicated that only the academic situations factor was accounted for by the greatest variance and had the highest reliability. This finding supports the research on the difficulties AD/HD individuals have in academic settings. **Even though an individual with AD/HD may have high intelligence, AD/HD symptoms make academic situations very challenging.** College students with AD/HD often report that teachers and parents have referred to them as underachievers with low motivation (Biggs, 1995).

Barkley Semi-Structured Interview

As most research suggests, one measurement does not make an accurate diagnosis of AD/HD. A more in-depth interview with the patient and more measures must be given to rule out the possibility of other psychological or physical disorders. The Barkley (1991) Semi-Structured Interview was included in the study to offer additional information about the individual's background.

Four participants from the Introductory Psychology control group met the *DSM-IV* criteria for the disorder. The semi-structured interview showed that the four individuals had problems with depression in the past. Since AD/HD has such a high rate of comorbidity, a semi-structured interview can help rule out the possibility of other psychological disorders before making a conclusion about a diagnosis of AD/HD.

DSM-IV Criteria Checklist

Six of 18 individuals with AD/HD did not meet the *DSM-IV* criteria for AD/HD. Since the criteria have not been adapted for adults, it is suggested that AD/HD can be diagnosed in individuals without the individual meeting the *DSM-IV* criteria. Only two of the six individuals were not taking medication. However, it could be inferred that the medications individuals with AD/HD were taking were very effective at lengthening attention levels and controlling impulsivity and other symptoms of the disorder.

ADDITIONAL CONCLUSIONS FROM THE STUDY

According to current research (Berry et al., 1995), it was suggested that men and women with AD/HD display different symptoms of the disorder. No significant gender differences were found. However, more women participated in the study than did men, which may have made it more difficult to detect gender differences.

The study concentrated primarily on college students. Only 4 of 82 participants were not college students. The second group of individuals with AD/HD, the adult group, was added to the study because of small sample size of participants with AD/HD. The adult group with AD/HD had significantly higher mean scores on both the Brown (1996) and Nadeau (1994) measures. Since the adults were solicited from a support group, they may have had more severe forms of the disorder.

The adult AD/HD group was much older than the college students with AD/HD. The mean age of the adults was 33 years, as opposed to 22 years of age for college students with AD/HD. The adults may have had more knowledge of the disorder and been more aware of the symptoms present in themselves. The adult AD/HD group was very small. Self-selection bias may have selected the most severe individuals.

College students with AD/HD who participated in the study may not have had as severe forms of the disorder, and may have developed successful coping strategies. Most of the individuals with the disorder were currently taking medications for their AD/HD. The college students with AD/HD were pooled from a highly selective, private, liberal arts college, and these students may have developed successful coping strategies so as to remain in a competitive academic environment. As the results indicated, there were significant differences between college students with AD/HD and both control groups for all three measures. These findings support evidence for the continuation of symptoms into adulthood.

It is important to note that there was a difference, although not significant, between the two control groups. The control group of Introductory Psychology students participated in a group setting. The participants received research credit and knew they had an hour to complete the questionnaire. The other control group was made up of volunteers randomly solicited from the library. Overall, the library control group responded more like the college students with AD/HD.

These results indicate that individuals solicited from the library tend to answer differently than students who were participating in the study for class credit. The participants from the library may have been more rushed. Most likely, the participants wanted to quickly finish the questionnaire so that they could do what they intended to do in the library in the first place. If levels of attention are being measured, it is suggested that the group administration with Introductory Psychology students may lead to more typical responses.

The sample size of students with AD/HD was quite small, and most participants were middle-to-high socioeconomic status. An expanded group of college students with AD/HD may give more weight to the results of this study. Further research should focus on a more diverse group of college students with AD/HD. Additionally, individuals with AD/HD may not have had very severe forms of the disorder, which may have affected the results of the study.

More research should be conducted on the validity and reliability of measures for diagnosing AD/HD in adults. Research needs to focus on how continuation of AD/HD symptoms affect adulthood. As Brown's ADD scale (Brown, 1996), Nadeau's College Level AD/HD Questionnaire (Nadeau, 1994), and the College Situations Questionnaire indicate, AD/HD can not be conceptualized by a specific set of criteria. There are a variety of symptoms in adults. As results of the present study suggest, valid measures should include a broader range of symptoms for the diagnosis of AD/HD in adults. Once AD/HD in adults is better understood, measures for diagnosing the disorder in adults can be given more validation for use in clinical settings.

References

American Psychiatric Association (1994). *Diagnostic and statistical manual of mental disorders. (4th ed).* Washington, DC: Author.

Barkley, R. A. (1990). *Attention deficit hyperactive disorder.* New York: Guilford Press.

Barkley, R.A. (1991). *Attention-deficit hyperactivity disorder: A clinical workbook.* New York: Guilford Press.

Berry, C.A., Shaywitz, S.E., & Shaywitz, B.A. (1985) Girls with attention deficit disorder: A silent minority? A report on behavioral and cognitive characteristics. *Pediatrics, 76,* 801-809.

Biggs, S. H. (1995). Neuropsychological and psychoeducational testing in the evaluation of the ADD adult (pp. 109-131). In K.G.Nadeau(Ed.), *A comprehensive guide to attention deficit disorder in adults: Research, diagnosis, and treatment.* New York, NY: Brunner/ Mazel.

Brown, T. E. (1995). Differential diagnosis of ADD versus AD/HD in adults. (pp.93-108). In K. G. Nadeau (Ed.), *A comprehensive guide to attention deficit disorder: Research, diagnosis, and treatment.* New York, NY: Brunner/ Mazel.

Brown, T. E. (1996). *Brown attention-deficit disorder scales.* The Psychological Corporation. San Antonio,TX: Harcourt Brace & Company.

Conners, C.K. (1985). The computerized continuous performance test. *Psychopharmacology Bulletin, 21,* 891-892.

DuPaul, G. J., (1990) The home and school situations questionnaires - revised: Normative data, reliability, and validity. Unpublished manuscript, University of Massachusetts Medical Center, Worcester.

Gittleman, R., Mannuzza, S., Shenker, R., & Bonagura, N. (1985). Hyperactive boys grown up. *Archives of General Psychiatry, 42,* 937-947.

Greenberg, M. S. (19930. Developmental normative data on the test of variables of attention (TOVA). *Journal of Child Psychology and Psychiatry and Allied Disciplines, 34,* 1019-1030.

Heiligenstein, E., & Keeling, R.P. (1995). Presentation of unrecognized attention deficit hyperactivity disorder in college students. *Journal of College Health, 43,* 226-228.

Javorsky, J. & Gussin, B. (1994). College students with attention deficit disorder: An overview and description of services. *Journal of College Student Development, 35,* 170-177.

Leimkuhler, M. E. (1994). Attention-deficit disorder in adults and adolescents:Cognitive, behavioral, and personality styles. In J.M. Ellison, C. S. Weinstein, & T. Hodel-Malinofsky (Eds.), T*he psychotherapists guide to neuropsychiatry: Diagnostic and treatment issues* (pp. 175-216). Washington, DC:Ameri -can Psychiatric Press.

Nadeau, K. (1994). How do you know if you have ADD? In P. O. Quinn (Ed.), *ADD and the college student* (pp. 7-18). New York: Magination Press.

Ratey, J.J. (1995). Special diagnostic and treatment considerations with women with attention deficit disorder. In K.G. Nadeau (Ed.), *A comprehensive guide to attention deficit disorder in adults: Research, diagnosis, and treatment* (pp. 260-283). New York, NY: Brunner/Mazel.

Sohlberg, M.M., & Mateer, C. A. (1987). Effectiveness of an attention-training program. *Journal of Clinical and Experimental Neuropsychology, 9,* 117-130.

Tzelepis, A., Schubiner, H., Warbasse, L.H. (1995). Differential diagnosis and psychiatric comorbidity patterns in adult attention deficit hyperactivity disorder. In K. G. Nadeau (Ed.), *A comprehensive guide to attention deficit disorder in adults: Research, diagnosis, and treatment* (pp. 35-57). New York, NY: Brunner/Mazel.

Wender, P. H., Reimherr, F. W., Wood, D. R. (1985). Psychopharmacological treatment of attention deficit disorder residual type (ADD, RT, minimum brain dysfunction, hyperactivity) in adults. *Psychopharmacology Bulletin, 21*, 222-231.

□

THE NEUROPSYCHOLOGICAL PROFILE OF THE STUDENT WITH AD/HD

James M. Sydnor-Greenberg, Ph.D.
Clinical Psychology and Neuropsychology
Clinical Instructor, Georgetown University

Neuropsychological testing assesses brain-behavior relationships, and helps fine tune evaluation of an individual's cognitive strengths and weaknesses. This testing should be included in the diagnostic work-up of AD/HD, and should be conducted while off stimulant medication. Cognitive testing for AD/HD includes assessment of attention, memory, intellectual aptitude, and executive functions. This article will review the following areas: neuropsychological assessment, and why it should be part of an AD/HD evaluation; testing on or off medication; attention testing; intelligence testing; memory testing; and, executive functions: what are they and how are they assessed? Use of neuropsychological assessment to guide recommended accommodations and strategies will also be addressed.

INTRODUCTION

What is Neuropsychological Assessment?

Neuropsychological assessment is the study of brain-behavior relationships. Neuropsychological tests offer a means to empirically assess virtually all cognitive functions including attention, memory, executive functions and reasoning skills, language and math abilities, visuospatial skills, and sensory-motor abilities. Neuropsychological testing differs from the medical neurological exam in that it is more detailed; assesses functions in greater depth; and provides statistically derived norms by which individuals can be compared to others their own age, gender, and educational level.

Why is Neuropsychological Assessment a Necessary Part of AD/HD Evaluations?

Neuropsychological testing provides additional data beyond interviews and rating scales. An AD/HD assessment need not include neuropsychological testing, but a thorough, cautious AD/HD assessment should include such testing. Many clinicians diagnose AD/HD based on interviews with the patient, family, and teachers; rating scales completed by the patient, family, and teachers; and in-office behavioral observations over the course of a relatively brief (one-to-two hour) interview. The problem with this type of an assessment is that alternative explanations for those symptoms that present as AD/HD are not addressed.

Interview and rating scales data can yield biased results. Many teachers over-diagnose AD/HD, in part because they are not aware of alternative explanations for disruptive behavior or inattention, and because they may be looking for a quick fix in the form of medication. Some parents share the same bias, while other parents do not want to believe their child could have a disorder and would instead like to blame the school or peers.

In each of these cases, rating scale data may simply reflect the bias of the rater. Also, a brief in-office assessment by the pediatrician may not allow enough time to observe the full repertoire of the patient, and often ratings scales overly influence the pediatrician.

Neuropsychological testing involves a detailed assessment of all cognitive functions, not just those related to attention, concentration, and processing speed. A neuropsychological battery may take four-to-six hours to administer, and includes a broad range of tasks. The psychologist has the opportunity to observe the patient over a lengthy period of time, and to observe the patient during a variety of simple, complex, short or long, easy or frustrating tasks. There is no agreed upon battery of tests for assessing AD/HD in adults (Biggs, 1995).

A selection of tests of attention, executive control, reasoning, and memory should be included in any evaluation. Tests to rule out other explanations of academic or vocational difficulties should also be included. Language, mathematics, visuospatial, and sensory-motor testing would complete a battery of tests.

Neuropsychological testing is useful to eliminate other cognitive or emotional disorders causing symptoms similar to AD/HD, or occurring comorbidly with AD/HD. To assess if a student has AD/HD, one must look for signs of core criteria symptoms such as inattention, hyperactivity, and impulsivity. Associated symptoms of AD/HD may often be misleading. For example, academics, self-esteem issues, and interpersonal problems are associated with AD/HD but also may be due to other disorders. The clinician must first determine presence of the criteria symptoms of AD/HD. Then, if associated symptoms are present, they may be explained as being related to the AD/HD or to some other factor.

There is an overlap between symptoms of AD/HD and language LD. For example, in both disorders individuals may complain of problems: absorbing information they hear in class; problems reading quickly; problems absorbing information the first time they read it; finishing written assignments on time; and organizing lengthy papers. However, students who have AD/HD without language LD, will not have problems with spelling, phonetic analysis, and other primary language skills. Students who have language LD without AD/HD, will not have attentional and executive function deficits. Use of psychoeducational achievement testing (e.g., Woodcock - Johnson Revised Achievement Battery) will easily address these issues.

There is also an overlap between some symptoms of AD/HD and Nonverbal LD, including problems with math, science, and poor social skills. However, students who have AD/HD without Nonverbal LD, will show no impairment on visuospatial tasks. Students who have Nonverbal LD without AD/HD, will not have attentional and executive dysfunction.

AD/HD without hyperactivity (ADD) and depression have overlapping symptoms of inattention, decreased motivation, sluggishness and hypoactivity. AD/HD with hyperactivity has similar symptoms to some anxiety disorders and hypomania. These include restlessness, racing thoughts, overactivity, impulsiveness, and impatience. One important distinction between AD/HD and these psychiatric disorders is that AD/HD is chronic, not episodic, and generally constant across situations.

Mood disorders are generally episodic, and anxiety may vary significantly across situations. A detailed, semi-structured, clinical interview of various psychiatric syndromes and the use of objective personality assessment (e.g., Minnesota Multiphasic Personality Inventory - 2, Beck Depression Inventory-II, and Beck Anxiety Inventory) is usually sufficient to rule out significant emotional factors.

Neuropsychological testing is needed to assess Executive Functions in detail. Rating scales typically only allude to executive function problems, and offer no objective means by which to assess such problems with self-regulation, planning, organization, and problem-solving. Executive functions are described in detail below.

Testing On or Off Medication?

Occasionally an individual is referred for neuropsychological testing after a pediatrician or psychiatrist has made a preliminary diagnosis of AD/HD and medication has already been prescribed. With the physician's permission, testing for AD/HD should be done with the patient off medication. This allows for the most accurate assessment of attention, memory, and executive function abilities.

There are times when a student is referred for neuropsychological testing to assess both AD/HD and LD issues. There is a high degree of comorbidity among these disorders. If a student is suspected of having both AD/HD and LD, the first task is to explore the AD/HD issues in detail. If the psychologist is comfortable with the diagnosis of AD/HD, the student can be referred back to the physician to discuss the efficacy of medication. After the medication has had a chance to minimize the effects of the AD/HD, the LD portion of the testing should be conducted. This allows for a more accurate assessment of academic achievement and past learning; the effects of poor concentration; and inconsistent and disorganized responding due to AD/HD.

Attention Testing

Individuals with AD/HD have specific difficulty with sustained attention and vigilance. This is especially true the longer the person must maintain attention, and when the presentation of material is examiner- paced, as opposed to self-paced (Pennington, 1991). Pennington (1991) cites studies that implicate right frontal lobe functioning in sustained attention.

There are a variety of **Continuous Performance Tests** that assess sustained attention and selective attention (the ability to maintain focus in the presence of distracters) (Biggs, 1995) including: the Gordon Diagnostic Systems; Conners' CPT; and the Test of Variables of Attention (TOVA). These tasks require the patient to monitor information that is presented over an extended time period.

For example, different paradigms of the GDS assess sustained visual attention, sustained auditory attention, sustained visual attention in the face of an auditory distraction, and sustained visual attention in the face of a visual distraction. Such tests measure inattention in the form of "misses" (not responding to a predetermined target stimuli) and "late responses". Impulsivity is measured in the form of "errors of commission" (incorrectly responding to something other than the predetermined target stimuli).

Visual Cancellation Tests have yielded mixed research findings in subjects with AD/HD. This involves paper and pencil testing in which the subject must cancel or circle a specified letter or shape on a page containing a variety of letters or shapes. Some studies found that AD/HD children demonstrate higher rates of commission errors (canceling letters or shapes other than the target). However, this is not always the case, especially when the task is self-paced.

A great deal of qualitative information can be gleaned from those tests. For example, impulsive patients often scan the page in an unstructured manner rather than scanning in rows or columns. Also, individuals with AD/HD generally have difficulty balancing speed and accuracy. Some individuals with AD/HD work too quickly and miss target stimuli (errors of omission) sacrificing accuracy for speed. Others who have learned to compensate for their tendency to make careless errors may work slowly and check their work over and over in order to be accurate, thereby sacrificing speed for accuracy.

Paced Auditory Serial Addition Test (Gronwall, 1977) measures divided and sustained attention but has been criticized because of its demands on arithmetic skills (Biggs, 1995).

Other tests of attention and memory seem not to be as affected by AD/HD including: rote auditory attention and concentration (e.g., Digit Span); story recall; and recall of spatial positions (Pennington, 1991). However, various conditions such as distracters, the number of items to be recalled, and processing speed can disrupt adequate functioning.

Intelligence Testing

The general intellectual functioning of individuals with AD/HD represents the full range of intelligence. However, "children with AD/HD may score somewhat lower on intelligence tests than control groups of children or even their own siblings" (Barkley, 1990, p. 632). Yet it is possible that in college, individuals with AD/HD may have particularly high intellectual levels, because getting to college may require not only great perseverance but a very high level of innate intelligence. It is well established that an individual can have AD/HD and be gifted intellectually. The use of a standard measure of intelligence, such as the WAIS-III, allows for a general assessment of a variety of verbal comprehension, perceptual organization, working memory, and processing speed skills.

The new **Wechsler Adult Intelligence Scale-III** (WAIS-III, 1997), includes new subtests and index scores that may be helpful in assessment of AD/HD, although controlled research still needs to be done. The validity of the "ACID" pattern of deficits in AD/HD (i.e., difficulty with Arithmetic, Coding (Digit Symbol on the WAIS-III) Information, and Digit Span) has been debated. This is because language and auditory processing deficits can also affect arithmetic, information, and digit span.

The WAIS-III has added a Working Memory Index (WMI, similar to the Freedom from Distractibility on the Wechsler Intelligence Scale for Children-III, 1991). This index consists of three subtests, Digit Span, Arithmetic, and Letter-Number Sequencing (LNS). LNS requires a great deal of mental control as the subject must listen to numbers and letters read in random order and the restate them by listing the numbers first in ascending order and then the letters in alphabetical order.

The clinician must be cautious in attributing a low WMI to AD/HD, as controlled research does not yet exist, and since Language LD and other auditory processing problems can not be ruled out. Anecdotally, the author has administered the WAIS-III to 22 college students and adults with AD/HD and executive dysfunction, and found that Arithmetic and Digit Span score vary but that LNS is uniformly problematic in AD/HD.

The WAIS-III has also added Symbol Search, which was first introduced on the WISC-III (1991). This task requires rapid comparing and contrasting of symbols, and along with Digit Symbol, can be used to yield a Processing Speed Index (PSI). There are no known published reports of the PSI in AD/HD. Anecdotally, the author's 22 above-mentioned AD/HD cases have varied in Digit Symbol scores but nearly all have had significant problems with Symbol Search. Controlled studies with larger samples are needed to assess the diagnostic utility of the WMI and PSI in AD/HD.

Qualitative analysis of the WAIS-III profile can yield interesting information. The subtests are constructed of items in ascending order of difficulty. Many individuals with AD/HD demonstrate intra-test scatter, meaning that they miss easy items and then correctly respond to more difficult items. Intra-test scatter may be due to carelessness; inability to consistently maintain concentration during testing; or inconsistent learning in school due to attentional lapses. Qualitative findings include the need to have instructions repeated, inattention to visual detail, tangential speech, and hyperverbalization (Biggs, 1995).

Memory Testing

Many individuals with AD/HD complain of poor memory skills. However, a distinction must be made between poor attention vs. poor memory, and between poor recall vs. poor retrieval of information from memory.

Attention vs. memory.

Some individuals complain they can not recall information with any accuracy or consistency, but in truth, they did not or could not pay close attention in the first place. Therefore, the information was never encoded into memory. A person with AD/HD may have excellent memory skills once information is attended to and encoded into memory.

Recognition vs. retrieval.

Other individuals with AD/HD complain that they can not access information even though they are sure they have learned it. Indeed such individuals do better with recognition tasks (e.g., multiple choice testing) than free recall (e.g., essay responses or short answer format). Often the difficulty with free recall or retrieval from memory is related to inability to cue oneself to access previously learned information. For example, a person may not be able to answer the question, "Who was President of the United States during the Civil War?", even though they are sure they learned this in the past.

Whereas, most know this information by rote, such rote recall may be deficient in AD/HD. The subject's recall may improve with cueing. Ask the subject, "What was one of the main issues in the Civil War?", and the subject may answer, "Freeing the slaves." Ask the subject, "Who freed the slaves?", and the subject may then correctly answer, "Abraham Lincoln." The subject was unable to perform that logical cueing mentally.

It is important to assess: initial recall as compared to delayed recall (how much gets into memory vs. how much is retained over time); and free recall vs. cued recall; and recall after repeated exposure to a stimuli (learning curve). Tests such as the Wechsler Memory Scale-III (1997) do both, and allow for assessment of auditory vs. visual memory.

What are Executive Functions and How are They Assessed?

Executive dysfunction is the most important cognitive deficiency in AD/HD, more important than impaired attention (Barkley, 1997). These functions will be described in detail below.

Executive Functions include:

- organization and planning of action over time;
- inhibition of impulsive action;
- set-maintenance and set-shifting (e.g., sticking with a successful problem-solving approach or developing an alternative approach if the first idea does not work);
- ability to mentally manipulate information and work with more than one set of information at a time;
- use of self-directed speech (Barkley, 1997) (or what others call sub-vocalization);
- ability to absorb new information in an organized, coherent manner;
- ability to draw on previously learned information to perform goal-directed activities (Barkley, 1997).

Barkley (1997) provides an extremely detailed explanation of executive function impairment in AD/HD. He has derived a new compelling theory of AD/HD as a disorder primarily of self-control, and not necessarily inattention, that has at its core executive dysfunction. Barkley's definition of executive functions is complex and generally includes the skills listed above. He defines these functions as "those self-directed actions of the individual that are being used to self-regulate" (Barkley, 1997, p. 56). They "occur during a delay in responding, that serve to modify the eventual response to an event, and that function to improve the long-term future consequences related to that event" (p. 56). In other words, executive functions are those cognitive functions that occur before the person responds to a stimulus.

One of the most influential researchers on executive skills, Martha Denckla (1991) discusses the overlap between Executive Dysfunction, which she describes as "assessment-derived and dimensional" (p.ix), and AD/HD which she described as "historically derived and categorical", (p. ix). She points out that the prefrontal cortex may be predominantly responsible for the cognitive dysfunction seen in AD/HD; but also notes the broader neurological underpinnings of AD/HD, which may include subcortical structures or dysfunction of the posterior right hemisphere attentional systems.

Specific Neuropsychological Tests of Executive Functions.

There are many tests that attempt to assess such functioning. **The Wisconsin Card Sorting Test** presents the patient with an interesting challenge to solve a problem (sorting cards by one of three basic principles), and then to shift problem-solving strategies based on feedback from the examiner. This test assesses:

-- how long it takes the student to develop one successful strategy;
-- how long it takes to come up with a second and third strategy to meet changing feedback from the environment;
-- how much the student will perseverate on an incorrect strategy despite repeated feedback that it no longer works (a lack of mental flexibility);
-- and if the student will be confused by am biguous feedback, lose mental set, and switch to a new strategy prematurely.

This test is scored for a variety of indicators, which allows the student to be compared to others his or her own age and education. Neuroimaging studies have implicated the role of the dorsolateral regions of the prefontal cortex in performing this task (Barkley, 1997).

The Stroop Color and Word Test assesses the ability to inhibit responding to interference while engaged in another task requiring self-control (Barkley, 1997). The Interference Trial of this task consists of showing the student a page in which words spelling one color name are written in the ink of another color (e.g., the word Red is written in blue ink). The student must say the color of the ink and resist the temptation to read the word.

The score on the Interference Trial is compared to a "predicted" score based on previously administered control trials to assess if the student is overly slowed down by this difficult task. The scores allow for inter-subject and intra-subject comparisons. That is, the person's scores are compared to a normative sample, and the person's scores on the three trials are compared to each other. Right prefrontal functioning has been implicated in neuroimaging studies (Barkley, 1997).

The Trail Making Test from the Halstead-Reitan Neuropsychological Battery assesses how well the student can work with two sets of information at one time. This test consists of two, connect-the-dot sequences of 25 items. Trails A, a sequence of numbers from 1-25, serves as a control. Trails B, requires the alternating of numbers and letters as follows: 1-A-2-B...13. The scores on each trial are compared to a normative sample and to each other, allowing for inter-subject and intra-subject comparisons.

Controlled Oral Word Association (verbal fluency, sometimes referred to as FAS) assesses processing speed on a task felt to be related to frontal lobe functioning. The student is asked to quickly state as many words as come to mind that begin with a certain letter for 60 seconds. This is done for three trials, typically for the letters F, A, and S. Percentile rank is assessed based on age and education.

These scores can also be compared to rapid naming of items belonging to a category (e.g., animals, job titles) which is felt to be more related to the language dominant temporal lobe providing an intra-subject comparison of a frontal-related task and a temporal lobe-related task.

Porteus Mazes (and other maze tests) have been linked to frontal lobe functioning. Such tasks require planning and assess impulsivity. Typically an individual is rated in terms of how many trials are needed to complete a maze without errors, or how many errors are made in completing the task.

Other tests that do not on the surface, seem to relate to attention, memory, or executive functions also may be helpful in an AD/HD assessment. **The Rey Osterrieth Complex Figure** is a complicated geometric design constructed around a main rectangle with inner and outer details. The patient is asked to copy this freehand. In order to copy this most efficiently and accurately it is helpful to draw the main rectangle first. Often individuals with AD/HD impulsively begin drawing one detail after the next without consideration of the main gestalt and produce distorted or out-of-proportion designs.

The Nelson-Denny Reading Test is normed from grade 9 to senior year of college. Although the vocabulary and reading comprehension subtests are designed to measure reading skills, the ability to obtain scores under timed -- and extended-time conditions makes them useful in assessment of AD/HD. For example, some AD/HD individuals read slowly and need to reread material not because of a primary language learning disability, but because of slow and disorganized encoding of new information. Such students work very slowly but accurately on tests of reading comprehension. The Nelson Denny will detect a pattern in which few questions are answered under timed conditions, but a high rate of accuracy is seen with extended time. The percentage of extra time needed may guide recommendations for academic and standardized test accommodations.

Using Neuropsychological Assessment to Guide Recommended Accommodations and Strategies

Testing can help delineate the individual's specific pattern of strengths and weaknesses. Individuals will work closer to their potential with different accommodations and strategies. Some need extra time on tests. The percentage of extra time needed to complete tasks, especially the Nelson-Denny Reading Test, is helpful in predicting the amount of extra time needed for in-class and standardized tests in high school and college. However, this test is too easy to provide useful prediction about the amount of extra time needed for a graduate or professional (e.g., law or medical school) student. Other students need multiple choice testing instead of essay testing due to problems with free recall of information.

Access to other students' notes after class, or permission to tape-record lectures to fill in gaps in their own notes, is helpful to students with slowed processing and problems listening and taking notes at the same time. Access to the lecturer's notes before class helps the student with very poor mental organizational skills get a sense of how various ideas and facts fit together.

Training in reading outlining techniques is also helpful to students with poor mental organizational techniques, as they may have problems differentiating essential versus nonessential detail. Paper-writing outlining techniques helps even the most creative student to present ideas logically and coherently. Coaching regarding general organization skills (Kristan, 1995) such as list making; use of a calendar or date book; and other time-management and prioritizing techniques are helpful to all students, but essential for the AD/HD student with executive dysfunction.

SUMMARY

Neuropsychological testing should be part of the evaluation for AD/HD. Such testing allows for a detailed assessment of different types of attention and memory skills, an evaluation of the student's intellectual aptitude, and assessment of executive functions. Testing can also provide elimination or an alternative explanation for AD/HD-like symptoms such as a learning disability or an emotional disorder. Finally, assessment can identify the student's cognitive strengths which can then be used to guide recommendations to accommodation the student's weaknesses.

References

Barkley, R.A. (1990). *Attention deficit hyperactivity disorder: A handbook for diagnosis and treatment.* New York: Guilford.

Barkley, R.A. (1997). *AD/HD and the nature of self-control.* New York: Guilford.

Biggs, S.H. (1995). Neuropsychological and psychoeducational testing in the evaluation of the ADD adult. In K. G. Nadeau (Ed.). *A comprehensive guide to attention deficit disorder in adults: Research, diagnosis, and treatment.* New York: Brunner/ Mazel.

Brown, J.I., Fishco, V.V., & Hanna, G. (1993). *Nelson-Denny reading test: Manual for scoring and interpretation.* Chicago: The Riverside Publishing Company.

Denckla, M.B. (1991). Foreword, in Pennington, B.F. *Diagnosing learning disorders.* New York: Guilford.

Douglas, V.I. (1988). Cognitive deficits in children with attention deficit disorder with hyperactivity. In L.M. Bloomingdale & J. Sergeant (Eds.). *Attention deficit disorder: Criteria, cognition, intervention.* New York: Pergamon Press.

Gronwall, D. (1977). Paced auditory serial addition task: A measure of recovery from concussion. *Perceptual and Motor Skills, 44,* 367-373.

Heaton, R.K., Chelune, G.J., Talley, J.L. Kay, G.G., & Curtiss, G. (1993). *Wisconsin card sorting test manual: Revised and expanded.* Odessa, FL: Psychological Assessment Resources.

Kristan, P. (1995). Getting it together: Notes from a personal organization skills consultant to adults with AD/HD. *The AD/HD Report,* Vol. Three, Number Three, June 1995.

Pennington, B.F. (1991). *Diagnosing learning disorders: A neuropsychological framework.* New York: Guilford.

Wechsler, D. (1991). *WISC-III: manual.* San Antonio: Harcourt, Brace, Jovanovich, Inc.

Wechsler, D. (1997). *WAIS-III: Administration and scoring manual.* San Antonio: Harcourt, Brace, & Company.

Wechsler, D. (1997). *WMS-III, Wechsler memory scale – third edition: Administration and scoring manual.* San Antonio: Harcourt Brace & Company.

☐

GENDER AND COMORBIDITY ISSUES: CONSIDERATIONS FOR SERVICE PROVIDERS

Lynne C. Shea, M.A.
Director, Women's Resource Center
Landmark College

The goal of this article is to provide information that will support service providers in considering how issues related to comorbidity and gender should shape their approach to students with AD/HD. The magnitude of the challenge posed by AD/HD, as the current generation of school-age children reaches adulthood, cannot be underestimated. Because AD/HD is comorbid (coexists) with more disorders than any other disorder, it is essential that anyone providing services to students with AD/HD, have a basic understanding of the various disorders most frequently associated with AD/HD. Colleges and universities must be prepared to deal with the challenges presented by individuals with attention disorders, to provide an effective program of services, for the sake of the students involved.

INTRODUCTION

Although it is only in the past decade that the nature and extent of Attention-Deficit/Hyperactivity Disorder (AD/HD) and its impact on institutions of higher learning in the United States has been recognized, the issues presented by AD/HD are now identified and inescapable. Challenges presented by students with attention deficits to postsecondary service providers can be great, and will only increase in the coming years as more and more school-age children diagnosed with AD/HD enter college. Given the dramatic increase in services offered on college campuses to support students with learning disabilities generally (Brinckerhoff, Shaw, & McGuire, 1993), it is especially important that service providers continue to develop ways to combine areas of expertise and prepare for even greater numbers in the next decade.

As our knowledge of AD/HD has developed, its prevalence within the adult population has become an increasing focus, both for researchers and in the popular press. With this new focus has come a rapidly expanding understanding of the factors involved in diagnosis and treatment of disorders of attention. A key component of this understanding is the exceptionally high degree to which AD/HD is comorbid with other disorders, including learning disabilities, as well as various psychological and emotional disorders.

Likewise, the role that gender plays in identification, evaluation, and treatment of individuals with AD/HD has recently received attention, with a growing recognition that the manifestation of AD/HD in women has been under-researched and under-represented in discussions of the topic (Gaub & Carlson, 1997; Ratey, Miller, &Nadeau, 1995).

Despite attention paid to the broad issue of comorbidity and specific factors related to gender, the complexities these two interconnected elements pose for diagnosis and treatment have not yet been adequately accounted for. This may be particularly true in terms of those working directly with students for three important reasons.

First, the provision of college services tends to be compartmentalized, spread across a number of professionals including learning specialists, ADA coordinators, residential and student services staff, counselors, and health services. This means that an individual whose attention disorder is accompanied for example, by a specific learning disability or an emotional-behavioral disorder, may need to seek services from several different sources that may be neither integrated nor coordinated.

Second, the diagnostic and treatment subtleties represented by issues of comorbidity and/or gender differences may exceed the level of training that any given service provider possesses. It is rare that a learning specialist, for example, has training in identifying and treating emotional disorders, or that a counselor has training in recognizing undiagnosed learning disabilities. The outcome is that a student who presents difficulties associated with AD/HD may have a major component of his or her difficulties overlooked in the process of seeking and receiving services.

The third factor is social or cultural in nature. Research advances and the expanding amount of information available through the popular media have meant increasing recognition and societal acceptance of AD/HD, and growing understanding of the problems associated with disorders of attention. But AD/HD is unique among disorders because of the extremely high frequency of associated difficulties, which is less widely known, understood, and accepted. Also, societal understanding of the subtle differences in how AD/HD is expressed in women lags well behind the general state of popular knowledge.

These cultural factors are exhibited in two ways. First, although AD/HD, through growing recognition and understanding has lost some of its stigma, most disorders with which it is comorbid continue to be stigmatized in the general culture. This is especially true of the psychological and emotional disorders often accompanying AD/HD. It is also true of the learning disabilities with which AD/HD may be associated, which after years of public education, can carry connotations of a lack of intelligence. Stigmas attached to the comorbid disorders make it more difficult for the student with AD/HD to accept that component of their difficulties when diagnosed, and to seek treatment. In a different but related fashion, the ways in which AD/HD is expressed symptomatically among women is often unrecognized or misdiagnosed based on cultural stereotypes, resulting in inappropriate treatment or no treatment.

COMORBIDITY

Previously, a central issue in the identifying and treating of AD/HD is that attention disorders can be comorbid with a great many other disorders. A sense of scale can be drawn from two statistics: Barkley (1990) has estimated that approximately 60 percent of boys who are diagnosed with AD/HD have accompanying conduct or oppositional defiant disorders; and that more than 50 percent of all individuals diagnosed with AD/HD also have another comorbid disorder (Brown, 1995; Tzelepis, Schubiner, Warbasse, 1995). In addition, research indicates that the symptoms of AD/HD can mask other disorders, such as anxiety disorders, or be entirely missed because of a comorbid diagnosis. This can be especially true for women, whose AD/HD symptoms often stem from internalizing rather externalizing behaviors, and may be misdiagnosed on that basis.

This discussion will not include other neurological disorders which must be ruled out in a diagnosis of AD/HD, such as Tourette's syndrome or epilepsy, nor will it cover acquired attention deficit syndrome as caused by head trauma or disease. Student services staff and other professionals might be aware of the existence of these other disorders or syndromes, but the focus here is on the more common conditions which frequently accompany AD/HD.

Conduct Disorders (CD) and Oppositional Defiant Disorder (ODD)

As stated above, conduct disorders are frequently comorbid with AD/HD, especially in boys. These individuals are typically identified early as "problem children" in school: they show evidence of antisocial behavior and generally "act out" at home or in school. As children or adults, these individuals are more likely to attract attention, to be referred for services, and to receive treatment. These conduct disorders predominantly affect males, and while the antisocial behavior attracts attention, learning difficulties can be ignored or attributed to this disruptive and impulsive behavior, rather than to a possible underlying attention deficit.

Conduct disorders in adults are referred to as the "antisocial personality disorder." Oppositional defiant disorder suggests less obvious externalized "acting out" behaviors. Individuals with this disorder are angry and less obvious in their opposition. It has been noted that the combination of a conduct disorder and AD/HD may be a true hybrid disorder, rather than primarily one or the other (Goldstein, 1997).

When individuals with a diagnosed behavioral disorder arrive at college, they are apt to struggle with: establishing social peer relationships; adapting to a code of socially normative behavior; and developing and exercising problem-solving skills and good judgment. In addition, if there is an identified or unidentified attention deficit, these students have often missed much of the content and skills development in secondary school typically necessary for success in college.

The transition to college may seem abrupt and extremely difficult, and these students especially are at risk for substance abuse and other high thrill and antisocial behaviors, including sexual promiscuity and vandalism. It is especially important that students with an identified psychological disorder be evaluated for underlying learning problems if they are experiencing difficulty in school.

Anxiety Disorders

The similarities between symptoms of attention deficit disorders and anxiety disorders may confuse the diagnosis of either, although the relationship between them is not clear-cut or uncontroversial. While the symptoms of inconsistent attention and restlessness can exist with both, individuals with anxiety disorders do not typically demonstrate the disinhibition, hyperactivity, impulsivity, poor sustained attention, or the "acting out" behaviors generally associated with AD/HD (Barkley, 1990). The prevalence of and possible underdiagnosis of AD/HD/Primarily Inattentive Type, and the emphasis given to impulsivity and hyperactivity on many rating scales, are areas requiring more discussion and research. Nonetheless, it is also clear that attention deficits can cause levels of anxiety that can interfere with both learning and daily life management, and it is essential that diagnostic criteria for both types of disorders be evaluated by a trained clinician.

Within this category, Obsessive Compulsive Disorder (OCD) is worthy of special mention. OCD and Obsessive Compulsive Personality Disorder (OCPD) can be distinguished from AD/HD in that symptoms differ in degree and in purpose (or lack thereof) of the obsessive activities. Both OCD and OCPD seem to suggest rigid and, often, secretive behaviors associated with rules or senseless but unavoidable impulses. The frequent perfectionism of the individual with AD/HD can lead to hyperfocusing on work, or compensatory strategies for organizing or restlessness, that may seem "compulsive."

In fact, references to obsession and compulsions may turn up in clinical evaluations or dialogues (Tzelepis, et al.,1995) of those with AD/HD, with "compulsive" being used for "impulsive" behaviors. However, OCD behaviors can be distinguished from preoccupations or impulsive behaviors associated with AD/HD—shopping, risk-taking behaviors, sexual promiscuity, or substance abuse—that seem to provide a temporary stress-relieving function. Although research does not suggest high comorbidity rate between AD/HD and OCD, they can coexist, and any evidence of compulsive behaviors or obsessive thinking recommends a thorough clinical evaluation.

Depression

The comorbidity rates with AD/HD for depression, dysthymia or other mood disorders are not agreed upon, and more research is needed in this area. While it has been suggested that depression is not more likely in AD/HD children as compared to "normal" children (Barkley, 1990), the similarities in symptoms can result in misdiagnosis. Although individuals with AD/HD may experience depressive mood swings, and those suffering from biological depression may exhibit impulsive, inattentive and associated behaviors, the two conditions are not the same and can be distinguished from one another in a clinical evaluation.

It is important to recognize that feelings of inadequacy, guilt, and anger directed inwards can result from undiagnosed attention deficit and lead to depressive symptoms. This can be especially true for women. Some research indicates that women with AD/HD may experience a greater degree of dysphoria and are more likely to be misdiagnosed with depression or underdiagnosed for AD/HD than men (Katz, Goldstein, & Geckle, in press).

Borderline personality disorders may also be mistaken for AD/HD, and vice versa, if one looks only at the evidence of mood swings, while not especially considering a complete history and, more significantly, the duration and intensity of the symptoms. Again, differential diagnosis for any of these disorders is complicated, and should only to be undertaken by a skilled clinician, preferably using a team approach.

Although beyond the scope of this article, it is worth mentioning that many of the disorders already discussed above may be comorbid with one another and that the relationship between disruptive behavior disorders and anxiety disorders is not fully understood (Goldstein, 1997). Accurate diagnosis may be complicated and call into question which disorders, including attention deficits, are primary and which are secondary.

Learning Disabilities

One frequent comorbid correlations with attention deficits is learning disability or language disorder. It is estimated that between 20 and 30 percent of individuals diagnosed with some form of learning disability also have AD/HD (Goldstein, 1997). The term "learning disabilities" has sometimes been used as a catchall, and may be defined differently based on context, i.e.., educational, clinical, or legal, and criteria used in that context. While it may be important to consider whether the associated learning disability is neurologically based such as dyslexia, or psychogenic and secondary to the attention disorder (e.g., in the case of a specific spelling or mathematics disability that stems from an underlying attention disorder), ultimately the question of etiology is secondary to the fact that a significant number of individuals with AD/HD also have learning problems extending beyond the impact their attention disorder has on learning. These disorders may include difficulties with reading or producing written language, difficulties with auditory processing or with oral expression, specific problems with arithmetic or more complex mathematics, and difficulties with high-order reasoning tasks.

Because AD/HD in itself will interfere with performance on academic tasks in areas such as: written production; reading rate and comprehension; auditory attention and processing; and organization, it may be difficult to distinguish a corollary learning disability in the case of an individual student with AD/HD. It is important to not assume that all of a student's academic difficulties stem from his/her attention disorder, and take into account possible impact of an associated learning disability, with all of its implications for treatment.

It is essential to recognize that many comorbid psychological disorders may also interfere with learning and can, in fact, contribute to difficulties in acquisition of language skills and knowledge. For example, obsessive-compulsive disorders may have a significant impact on an individual's ability to complete reading and writing assignments, and depression may significantly affect academic performance. This is why a team approach to evaluation and provision of services is so important. Not only must it be determined whether or not an individual has a learning disability in conjunction with AD/HD; it is also vital in recognizing the way in which associated emotional and psychological disorders may impede learning and academic performance.

For young adults, the transition to college in itself represents an enormous challenge. This is not simply because of the increased level of academic demand represented by coursework. College also requires students to adapt to a much greater level of independence, both academically and socially, and to negotiate this new freedom with far fewer support systems available.

Lack of the structures provided by living at home and by high school scheduling and curriculum may have a significant, negative impact on students with AD/HD. For individuals with AD/HD who also have learning disabilities, the combination of increased academic demands and reduced structure may be particularly devastating. It is vital that those working in colleges recognize the need for students with AD/HD to find effective structures and self-monitoring strategies, and to consider the likelihood that such students may also have learning disabilities that requiring academic support.

GENDER AND AD/HD

Identification and differential diagnosis of individuals with AD/HD is exceedingly complicated, but the role that gender plays in these areas adds another layer of complexity. A research review by Gaub and Carlson (1997) indicates that while males with AD/HD are more likely than females to develop comorbid conduct disorders and antisocial behaviors, women with AD/HD are at greater risk for depression, anxiety disorders, and learning problems and cognitive disorders.

These different patterns of comorbidity become significant in the context of college-age students who may have been recently diagnosed with AD/HD, or who may not have a diagnosis, but encounter sufficient difficulty in their first year in college to be referred for evaluation or academic assistance.

The likelihood that college-age women with AD/HD will be misidentified with a diagnosis of depression, anxiety disorder, or learning disability substituting for or superceding a diagnosis of attention disorder, cannot be discounted. While comorbid disorders most associated with males who have AD/HD may correlate with popular conceptions of AD/HD and contribute seamlessly to the diagnostic picture, those disorders associated more with women who have AD/HD can mask attention disorders and make a fully accurate identification of need more difficult.

If we see AD/HD as a puzzle, then difficulties diagnosing women reflect a frequent misfit of a piece of the puzzle or a misinterpretation of the picture entirely. Comorbid disorders can be mistaken for AD/HD; conversely, AD/HD can be mistaken for another disorder or a coexisting disorder, if a complete history and evaluation is not considered. This occurs because AD/HD can manifest itself differently in women and, from a societal perspective, symptoms can be perceived differently in women and in men.

With antisocial personality disorders, it is important to recognize that "antisocial" behavior is entirely contextual and runs along a continuum. Within our culture, the expectations for social behavior change as children grow up, and differs for males and females. For example, sexual promiscuity in college can be viewed negatively when associated with women, damaging to their social reputation, and positively for men who are "sowing their oats" and actually increasing their social esteem. Therefore, it is essential that any "antisocial" behavior be viewed in conjunction with other, more objective information, and that deviance from a subjective norm be considered carefully.

Research by Anderson (1997) supports the idea that girls are less frequently referred for special education services generally, and we anticipate that, because hyperactivity and disruptive behaviors are symptoms most likely to result in referral by teachers, girls who have AD/HD Type III, primarily inattentive, are often missed (Arnold, 1996). This "silent minority" (Berry, Shaywitz, & Shaywitz, 1985) can quietly move through school into college classrooms without the noticeable behavior traits of their male peers, but with the cognitive deficits and underdeveloped social skills that lead to low self-esteem and academic failure.

While a lack of research on girls and women with AD/HD has resulted in more questions than conclusions regarding distribution of subtypes of AD/HD by gender, and possible differences in treatment, recent discussions (see Katz, et al.; Solden, 1995; Ratey, Miller, Nadeau, 1995) suggest that the syndrome can manifest differently in women.

More research in this area is necessary, especially given that conservative estimates indicate that there are over a million girls and women with AD/HD in the United States (Arnold, 1996). It has been suggested that until the diagnostic criteria for detecting AD/HD, especially Type III, in girls and women is changed to reflect different degrees of symptoms, girls and women may continue to be underdiagnosed (Quinn & Nadeau, 1998; Arnold, 1996).

While some research suggests that for girls with AD/HD, peer relationships can be more difficult and academic failure more severe (Berry, et al., 1985), perhaps a more significant area for discussion might be societal expectations for women that make AD/HD both so debilitating yet almost "acceptable" with respect to symptoms. To an extent, young women moving from adolescence to adulthood, living away from home in a permissive environment requiring both independence and self-control, are expected to experiment with sexuality and substances, to demonstrate mood swings and impulsivity and, yet, to maintain some elements of control.

Likewise, for young women to have a history of "depression" combined with academic failure is not unusual, and does not always necessarily result in thorough evaluation. An aura of sadness or feelings of not being in control of one's life, which can be so profound in a woman with AD/HD, can be misidentified as depression or worse, as simply part of the pangs of "growing up."

An additional source of sadness or depression may lie in the sense of guilt and blame many girls and women may feel in not measuring up to societal expectations related to roles of caretaking and nurturing. Women often are expected to play specific roles in their relationships with others, whether parents, siblings, significant others or children. Women with AD/HD can fail to achieve or fulfill the expectations of these bonds and relationships, and consequently feel disconnected, incapable of achieving self-esteem and strong relationships without self-understanding. All these issues can add to the symptomatic picture presented by women with AD/HD, and further lead to misdiagnosis or under-identification.

THE ROLE OF SERVICE PROVIDERS

For individuals with AD/HD to receive adequate services at college, all of the factors discussed must be taken into account. All those involved in direct service delivery to students with AD/HD must understand and have working knowledge of the ways in which comorbidity and gender work into the equation, and use this knowledge to assure that services provided are adequately comprehensive.

Because many individuals with AD/HD are undiagnosed when they arrive at college, and because both gender and comorbid disorders make the diagnostic picture complex, it is especially important that a strong screening and referral for evaluation system is in place. The broad range of potential learning and emotional or psychological issues associated with AD/HD also highlights the need for a team approach, one integrating the expertise of college counselors, disability support staff, residential and student services, and health services.

When working with a student in danger of academic failure or experiencing clear psychological difficulty, the question of whether AD/HD is involved must certainly be considered, along with other potential causes. It is even more important, in considering the role that AD/HD may be playing in a student's difficulty, that other linked disorders be considered as well.

The starting point for addressing issues outlined here is to start from a mutual awareness of difficulties involved, and to take a comprehensive, integrated team approach to working with students who present multiple issues. Because the ability of individual service providers to share information and work collaboratively depends on the willingness of students to waive confidentiality rights and allow for sharing of information, using a truly integrated approach to support and intervention can be difficult. However, it is within the capacity of any postsecondary institution to create models of cross-departmental communication, integration, and training that allow a team approach.

Learning specialists need to become better informed about the nature of specific emotional and psychological disorders accompanying AD/HD, and to develop protocols suggesting when a student might consider accessing counseling or health services. Those in the counseling or health professions should become familiar with language-based difficulties that may be linked to AD/HD, and learn to recognize them in action (for example, the way in which an expressive language difficulty, such as word-retrieval problems, may appear as emotional issues). Those working with students in residence halls need to be informed about social and emotional issues that may accompany AD/HD, and develop strategies for dealing with obsessive-compulsive personality or anxiety disorders.

It is assumed in this article that the work of any individual or team of providers should be informed of how issues of gender and comorbidity are involved in AD/HD. Perhaps the most important point is to incorporate knowledge of the potential for a dual diagnosis in working with any individual identified as having AD/HD, and to assure that screening, evaluation, and treatment all take this potential into account. The potential for underidentifying and/or misdiagnosing arising from the complex factors of comorbidity and gender should also be considered in screening and evaluation when students present with other identified problems or with difficulties of an unspecified nature.

There is often a significant stigma attached to many of the potential comorbid disorders. It is vital that service providers be aware of this potential for stigma, and incorporate effective ways of helping students to understand their difficulties in objective, nonjudgmental terms. Helping students who may have multiple disorders come to terms with all of their needs must be seen as a vital component of this work.

A central consideration is how services are provided to students whose actions may include antisocial behavior such as lying, cheating, defiance, severe disorganization and "sloppiness," substance abuse, and other problems often dealt with in moral or punitive terms. Recognizing that such symptom patterns arise from specific disorders, and often are beyond the control or choice of the individual, is vital that moral judgment be set aside in working with such issues. This is particularly important in the case of learning specialists or residential staff who may be typically accustomed to dealing with such behavior in ethical rather than clinical terms. It is essential that understanding not be enabling, and that clear expectations for personal responsibility and accountability be maintained.

It is rare that a student with AD/HD has solely academic issues, or has academic issues arising solely from his or her AD/HD without an accompanying learning problem. It is essential that residential staff, most often at the point of first contact with a student, have an understanding of the nonacademic effects of AD/HD and the potential corollary disorders that a student may have, so that they can provide early recognition of potential problems. They must know about other services available to a student and how they are accessed, so that students can be steered in the right direction. A team approach with significant discussion and cross-training across departments may be of significant aid. Those providing academic services or working with students in related contexts, must be careful to look for signs that an individual's AD/HD is associated with a learning disability, and be careful to provide information about how to seek a fuller educational assessment if needed.

In addition to issues related to comorbidity, there are some special considerations related to gender. It is vital that AD/HD and comorbid diagnoses not be missed or mistaken for one another. Given the correlations between CD/ODD and AD/HD in boys, it is essential to recognize what happens when these boys "grow up". Some difficulties that a male with AD/HD is experiencing may be linked to other disorders. These behaviors may include challenging rules and authority figures, vandalism, substance abuse, and excessive risk-taking.

For girls and women, it is first vital to question whether AD/HD is the issue when an individual presents with academic difficulties or other problems. The under-recognition of girls with AD/HD means that an interview with a postsecondary academic support person is the first opportunity a young woman may have to identify the true source of her problems. In addition, the importance of not mistaking AD/HD for depression while recognizing that it can coexist is central.

The sadness, low self-esteem and mood changes that can characterize AD/HD, unaccompanied by impulsivity or hyperactivity, can be frequently identified as depression. If so treated, medication and therapy will no doubt be ineffective in alleviating difficulties of inconsistent attention and disorganization that may result in a depressed affect.

For both genders, there is a need for better screening techniques and inventories that can help distinguish between common symptoms and their potential causes and encourage further evaluation for potential coexisting conditions. It is important that clinicians and academic support personnel recognize that AD/HD can, in fact, become a desired diagnosis by some in denial about other conditions which carry more stigma or present a more complex and difficult diagnosis.

CONCLUSION

Ultimately, issues of gender and comorbidity add to the puzzle that is AD/HD. For women, the key pieces are often missing, or misidentified. For men, certain patterns of behavior are often accurately recognized, but other equally important pieces overlooked. The likelihood for any individual with AD/HD is that some other disorder coexists. For a woman with AD/HD, it is likely that her attention disorder has not been recognized, or has been misdiagnosed. For both genders, the very real possibility of an associated learning disability or of a comorbid psychological disorder is all too often discounted or disregarded. For men and women with AD/HD to receive all of the services that they need and are entitled to, this situation must change.

References

Anderson, K.G. (1997). Gender bias and special education referrals. *Annals of Dyslexia, 7,*151-161.

Arnold, L.E. (1996) Sex differences in ADHD: Conference summary. *Journal of Abnormal Child Psychology, 24* (5) 555-569.

Barkley, R.A. (1990) *Attention deficit hyperactivity disorder: A handbook for diagnosis and treatment.* New York: Guilford Press.

Berry, C.A., Shaywitz, S.E., Shaywitz, B.A. (1985). Girls with attention deficit disorder: A silent minority? A report on behavioral and cognitive characteristics. *Pediatrics, 76(*5): 801-809.

Brinckerhoff, L.C., Shaw, S.F., McGuire, J.M. (1993). *Promoting postsecondary education for students with learning disabilities.* Austin, TX: Pro-Ed.

Brown, T.E. (1995). Differential diagnosis of ADD versus ADHD in adults. In K.G. Nadeau (Ed.), *A comprehensive guide to attention deficit disorders in adults: Research, diagnosis, and treatment,* 93-108. New York: Brunner/Mazel.

Gaub, M., & Carlson, C.L. (1997) Gender differences in ADHD: A meta-analysis and critical review. *Journal of the American Academy of Child and Adolescent Psychiatry, 36:*8, 1036-1045.

Goldstein, S. (1997) *Managing attention and learning disorders in late adolescence & adulthood: A guide for practitioners.* New York:John Wiley & Sons.

Katz, L.J., Goldstein, G., Geckle, M. (in press). Neuropsychological and personality differences between men and women with ADHD. *Journal of Attention Disorders.*

Quinn, P.O., Nadeau, K.G. (1998). Gender issues and attention deficit disorder. *The ADHD Challenge (12),* 2.

Ratey, J.J., Miller, A.C., Nadeau, K.G. (1995) Special diagnostic and treatment considerations in women with attention deficit disorder. In K.G. Nadeau (Ed.), *A comprehensive guide to attention deficit disorders in adults: Research, diagnosis, and treatment* 260-283. New York: Brunner/Mazel.

Solden, S. (1995). *Women with attention deficit disorder.* Grass Valley, CA: Underwood Books.

Tzelepis, A., Schubiner, H., & Warbusse, L.H.III (1995). Differential diagnosis and psychiatric comorbidity patterns in adult attention deficit disorder. In K.G. Nadeau (Ed.), *A comprehensive guide to attention deficit disorders in adults: Research, diagnosis, and treatment* 35-57. New York: Brunner/ Mazel.

☐

ADDITIONAL RISKS FACING COLLEGE STUDENTS WITH AD/HD

Patrick J. Kilcarr, Ph.D.
Director, The Center for Personal Development
Georgetown University

The following article explores the strength of the relationship between college students with AD/HD and the abusive use of alcohol and other drugs. College students who have AD/HD will describe their feelings and ability to handle alcohol, and other drug-related issues. Further discussions include the need for universities and colleges to create a protective and positive environment for facilitating educational success of students living with learning disabilities and/or AD/HD.

INTRODUCTION

While true that we now know a great deal about AD/HD and its influence on behavior, there is still a vast amount we don't know about the relationship between AD/HD and use of substances during college. It is hypothesized that use of alcohol and other drugs during college is closely linked to the frequency, duration, and intensity of treatment the person received during his or her younger years.

Those entering college with undiagnosed AD/HD may find use of alcohol and/or other drugs produces the dual effect of temporarily reducing stress, while simultaneously increasing a general sense of euphoria. This can become emotionally and socially reinforcing, resulting in the individual pursuing more opportunities to drink and/or use illicit substances.

Receiving early intervention is thought to be an important, protective mechanism against problems in adolescence and adulthood. It is not clear, however, that there is a direct relationship between early intervention and use and/or abuse of substances in college. One student noted:

> **I went to private school since the third grade. This particular school specialized in dealing with kids who had learning problems and hyperactivity. I saw a counselor weekly and my parents were very supportive of me. I do feel I had a lot of support growing up. When I came to college I began using pot. At first it was occasional, then over time I relied on it more and more. I liked how**

it made me feel. I didn't worry or doubt after I smoked-up. Obviously, I didn't really see what it was doing to my academic life and relationships with other people. I began caring less about things and hanging almost exclusively around kids who smoked-up. I guess I am lucky that one of my professors brought my absences and endless excuses to the Dean. She sat me down and said I had to let my parents know what was going on, because I was failing the semester. I probably didn't have to tell my parents anything really. I could have lied. But inside I could see that things weren't right. I also knew I was going to have to take a semester off from school anyway, so I started going to treatment back home.

I don't really know what would have made a difference for me in terms of using pot. Maybe my parents holding me more accountable during my first year of school. I am sure I would have resented them being involved in my life once I was off to school. They felt I needed space to experience college without them breathing down my neck. Based on my history and pretty impulsive behavior, a closer monitoring may have helped, or made me more vigilant about what I was doing.

Addressing many of the negative attributes associated with AD/HD early in a child's life has a tendency to foster acquisition of fundamental coping strategies and behaviors that make individuals with AD/HD more resilient and less at risk. Monitoring the child's behavior and choices, especially during early school years, can help extend these strategies into the college environment. These strategies become instrumental in college, which places enormous demand on an individual's ability to attend, follow rule-governed behavior, and accomplish significant academic requirements.

Anecdotally, adults who experienced early diagnosis and treatment, seemed to experience fewer problems directly associated with AD/HD. General coping strategies, combined with a greater sense of personal control and mastery over social situations, seems to be an essential mitigating factor in reducing excessive need for, or use of alcohol and other drugs. As one student explained:

I entered college feeling pretty good about who I was as a person. I have to deal with a lot in my life. School has never come particularly easy, so I had to combine discipline with some sound guidelines. I owe this thinking to my parents who hooked me up with some great coaches. These various people cheered me on toward success. I learned what it was going to take for me to make it. It also meant I had to have a vision about what I wanted. Part of that vision did not include getting wasted on drugs or booze. I knew up front before I began school. I do drink, but I am clear about what I want. I feel good about myself, and I really feel good when I leave a party or social scene and I know what I am doing and who I am with... It used to be that I had to make life adjust to my ADD. But you know, when I look at some of my friends here at school, who haven't had to confront the stuff I have had to, I see myself and my choices way out ahead.

There also appears to be a connection between a student's perception of available academic resources at college and his/her use of alcohol and other drugs. Students who have greater access to learning services and academic support to help manage AD/HD-related issues, tend to experience concomitantly lower levels of stress and substance abuse. Consequently, colleges can play an integral role in helping to foster academic and social success of students who have AD/HD.

Learning Services coordinators need to let students know up-front what services are available, and what would impede students' use of learning resources. Students who have received a great deal of attention to their respective learning impairment during the course of their life may enter college believing they have received everything they need to be academically and socially competent.

One of the most accurate barometers of a student's progress is asking how he or she is doing socially, and with respect to overall course work. Individuals who are overextended socially may find their academic performance suffering. Supporting students in balancing and developing manageable strategies can increase student ownership of the issue, thus reducing the problem.

When students aren't interested in exploring their problem behaviors, referring them to the counseling center and/or the on-campus alcohol and other drugs program, may be the only recourse. As one learning services coordinator described:

I meet the students where they are at and encourage them to become proactive in terms of their learning experience. If I see a student is struggling with alcohol, depression, etc., I attempt to raise their consciousness to the problem and suggest meeting with a counselor to discuss what is going on. I don't hit them over the head with it; I gently, yet firmly acknowledge that whatever is going on is dragging them down. This means they are not able to function at their optimum level.

No one likes to be told they are having a problem. Especially students who have struggled years with various learning issues. They want so desperately to perform well and be a success. This is often the carrot I use to have them at least see a counselor. It takes courage to admit that something is out-of-control. I see enormous courage in our students, regardless of whether or not they are having problems with alcohol or drugs.

It is also important to have a sound working relationship with the university's counseling center. I know the counselors, and feel comfortable referring students to them and collaborating regarding what is in the best interest of the students. This relationship has proved invaluable for a number of our students who periodically lose their way or find they have fallen way off the path.

TRACKING VULNERABILITY

AD/HD does not increase an individual's susceptibility to developing a substance abuse problem (Weiss & Hectman, 1993). Emergence of secondary problems related to primary issues associated with AD/HD: consistent negative feedback from the environment, relative to the ongoing impulsivity and lack of personal control; diminished academic performance due to inattentiveness in class; and strained social relations due to ceaseless restlessness and distractibility are more likely to increase susceptibility.

AD/HD is often influenced by social feedback and scrutiny. Unlike a learning disability which can be largely confined to the world of academics and managed through hard work and accurate learning strategies, AD/HD impacts all aspects of the individual's life: academic, social, emotional, psychological, and spiritual. The impetus of AD/HD can propel an individual into the world like a child racing helplessly down a snow clad hill on a saucer - completely at the mercy of gravity and good fortune. The point of intervention, when the individual begins to regain a sense of personal control over the plummet, has marked influence on the overall manifestation of AD/HD-related problems.

The later the intervention, the greater the individual's exposure to noxious feedback and internalized negative feelings, about self. The more intense the negative feelings, the deeper and more constant the resultant emotional pain. It is often in the desire to reduce the pain and seek temporary asylum from AD/HD-related problems that college students discover the benefits of self-medicating through alcohol or other drug use. Intuitively, we know that this merely serves to ultimately increase the individual's pain and reduce personal control. However, for someone in a relative state of emotional pain or angst, they may not comprehend the long-term impact of their immediate-use patterns. As one student noted:

> **I have always had this furrowed brow. People forever have commented on it; saying I look terminally perplexed or confused. I think of it as my 'worry repository'. Things have never seemed very easy. I worry a lot and am anxious a lot. I worry I am not going to do the right thing, say the right thing, or worse say or do the wrong thing. I experimented in high school with beer. But once I got to college, the rule book about drinking or whatever was left behind. I found that drinking let me unwind...relax. I didn't take things, especially me, so serious...The problem was that I wanted to feel that way all the time. I waded too far out and, before I knew it, I was being swept away.**
>
> **It is only recently that I have begun sorting out the meaning of ADD in my life, and the very real impression it has had on me. I am a very smart person; the tests I have taken even indicate this. But I do not feel very smart. One day I can do no wrong, the next day I can do no right. It's not easy because I have grown used to finding something outside myself to control my inner stuff. I did not come to college prepared to handle college situations let alone all my personal needs. I am learning. It would have been nice to understand a lot of this before coming here.**

What do we do as a university or college when we receive talented, bright, and gifted students with AD/HD and/or LD who perceive themselves as damaged goods? They tend to focus on the tear in the fabric rather than the fabric as a whole. It's a great challenge to academic institutions to create a safety net that will identify and catch these students before they destroy their academic potential through substance abuse.

THE COLLEGE ENVIRONMENT

College is a time of extraordinary growth in the life of an individual. Values and ethics which were foundational while growing up are now questioned and challenged. Participation in religious practices important to the family of origin may wane during this time. The college student is no longer a child, and yet, is not fully an adult either. The individual is struggling to make sense out of life during the "between time"; a time where experimentation is critical to the overall development of the person. Formal guidance on the importance of experimenting in college is often nominally present, or missing altogether. Very few colleges actually have ongoing programs or courses that explore developmental imperatives facing college students.

Experimenting, especially with alcohol and other drugs during this time, can be dangerous. It's most dangerous for individuals having difficulty accurately regulating their impulsivity, and demonstrating consistent appropriate risk-taking behavior. Use of substances in a largely unregulated environment like college, can present unique challenges to individuals with AD/HD.

AD/HD AND COLLEGE

While we can never know for certain which individual with AD/HD is at risk for substance abuse, it's clear that AD/HD places him/her at higher risk for substance abuse problems. The combination of emotional stability and degree of impulsivity can often determine the level-of-risk confronting the student. Low self-esteem, combined with high impulsivity, has a tendency to increase a student's risk for substance-abuse problems. According to Weiss & Hechtman (1993) and Feldman et al., (1979), AD/HD is considerably overrepresented in individuals with substance-abuse problems. This is probably associated with an attempt to self-medicate symptoms linked to AD/HD, i.e., low-self esteem, anxiety, emotional pain, etc.

College is often a time when students with AD/HD have unrestricted and largely unregulated access to alcohol and other drugs. College socializing frequently involves the presence of large amounts of alcohol, with heavy consumption encouraged. These particular socializing rituals combined with AD/HD can be a problem.

It is assumed that students entering college, who have had long-term exposure to multimodal therapy (counseling, medication, social skills groups, and positive educational experiences) seem to respond to alcohol-related issues similar to their non-AD/HD college peers. This is anecdotally based on conversations with colleagues working closely with college students presenting with AD/HD-related issues. This can also be extrapolated from the research of Satterfield et al., (1988), who noted that adolescents receiving multimodal therapy had fewer AD/HD issues than those receiving no intervention, or medication alone.

It seems the key to developing resiliency in a child with AD/HD is to provide him/her with many opportunities directed toward experiencing personal success. Success being defined as anything the child considers pro-social and positive. Feeling positive is one of the main ingredients to elevated self-esteem.

What happens if an individual enters college with Attention Deficit Disorder that has either gone undiagnosed or received little professional attention? The combination of academic and social pressure may overwhelm the coping strategies the student with AD/HD has relied upon during childhood and high school. This pressure may result in poor decision-making regarding use of alcohol and other drugs. It could also result in the student feeling a certain degree of hopelessness or helplessness, resulting in quitting school. As noted earlier, students with AD/HD may engage in, or increase their alcohol or other drug consumption to reduce stress, and to feel socially allied with his/her peers. The increased use of substances can seriously increase the student's risk for academic and social problems.

PREVENTATIVE MEASURES

One of the greatest sources of prevention that needs to occur **before** someone with AD/HD leaves for college is a frank discussion by parents, teachers, and/or counselors (when appropriate) regarding the many different situations the student will encounter, and the many decisions he/she will need to make. One college sophomore, who was diagnosed with AD/HD at age 10, gives his perspective on the whole concept of "preparing" for college.

> **Preparing for college was important for me. I find transitions somewhat overwhelming. And when I don't prepare, I have a tendency to make poor decisions. My high school offered a workshop on anticipating college life. In fact, that is what it was called. The class lasted for three weeks, meeting for three hours each time. At the time, it was a pain to go.**
>
> **Now that I am in school, it has made a huge difference on almost every level. I use the learning services department at school for all sorts of things; developing successful leaning skills to help put together the best academic schedule for me. I am also an athlete at the university, so these resources have made all the difference for me. Having support really helps me. I am not too proud to ask for help, because I know when I do, things usually work out in my favor.**

When our students enter college without this level of preparation, it becomes our responsibility to recognize when students are in trouble and to provide necessary resources. Individuals entering college with AD/HD need to know up-front the services and resources provided by the institution they will be attending. It is better to have the resources available and not need them, than to need them and not have them. Learning services coordinators can consider some of the following questions regarding the institution's ability and willingness to deal with issues specific to AD/HD.

Does the institution have a "learning services" program which can address specific issues related to AD/HD?

What is the extent of these services? Does the university provide students with AD/HD comparable services offered students with L.D., i.e., untimed testing, tutorial support with reading and writing assignments, etc.

What is the prevailing attitude on campus by academic staff regarding AD/HD? Are they receptive to the advice of the learning services coordinator regarding specific needs of the student? How does the coordinator handle unresponsive academic staff?

Is there ongoing testing and evaluation available to students who present with further academic problems?

If the learning services program is in its formative stages or underfunded (which is often the case), what are other universities of comparable size and funding ability doing? Benchmarking existing college programs is a wonderful way of networking, not recreating the wheel, and gauging how other colleges develop partnerships and use scarce funding resources.

These questions can certainly help coordinators maximize their time while zeroing in on critical issues confronting students with AD/HD on college campuses. If services and support needed are unavailable, the greater the risk students with AD/HD may develop a negative relationship with alcohol and other drugs.

It has been my experience that coordinators and counselors involved in learning services address the impact of college on the "whole" person. This means showing interest in, and getting information about their academic, social, and emotional functioning. Some of the best learning services coordinators I have seen in many ways resemble a winning coach. This concept was eloquently stated by a woman who has struggled most of her life with LD and ADD:

> **I was worried about going to college. Very little has worried me more in my life. During my initial visit to the school, I was invited to meet the director of the LD Support Program for the college. I remember sitting down, kind of nervous, and feeling like my great secret was on display for everyone. That's just how I remember feeling. Anyway, she sat next to me and said, with a big warm grin, "You are about to enter one of the most exciting and rewarding experiences of your life, and I hope you come here so I can celebrate your victories with you." What an incredible thing to say, especially to a scared-unsure kid. Ever since coming here, everyone involved in the L.D. Program has been the greatest source of support I could have imagined. It's a partnership. They don't things for, they do things with me, and encourage me to lead the way. I feel remarkably lucky.**

INTERVENTION

It is essential for Learning Services coordinators to know how to identify and refer a student struggling with an alcohol or other drug problem. The following vignette succinctly describes what to do when a student is in trouble:

> **I had been following a student named Steve for some time. Toward the end of October, I noticed he was either not coming to his scheduled sessions, or he was arriving late and leaving early. He seemed distant and uninterested. This was a marked change from his previous behavior.**
>
> **One evening, he arrived halfway through a writing class and was preparing to leave twenty minutes later. I met him in the hallway and expressed my concern about his attendance and apparent disinterest in the services offered. He looked at me sleepily and said he had been busy. As he was speaking, I began to smell alcohol. I asked if he had been drinking, and he said he had a beer with a friend at dinner. I invited him to come and see me the next day, to which he agreed. Steve never did show up to the meeting and dropped out of Learning Services altogether.**
>
> **I phoned his dean and expressed my concern and wondered how he was doing in his academic classes. The dean called me back later that day and indicated he was almost failing his courses for lack of attendance. The dean called Steve in and suggested that his behavior indicated he was in trouble. He mentioned that I had smelled alcohol during the previous week, and he pointed out that attending an academic function after drinking was a sign of a problem.**
>
> **After much talking, Steve admitted to spending almost all of his time and money on partying. He felt he had dug**

himself into a huge hole which he could not get out of. The dean contacted the counseling center, which houses our substance abuse program. He sent Steve over for an alcohol and other-drug evaluation. Steve felt connected to the counselor he met, and began the process whereby he had to seriously assess the detrimental effect alcohol has had on his life. His therapist contacted the dean and stated that his academic problems were the direct result of a severe alcohol problem. The professors were contacted, and Steve had the option of receiving a medical leave of absence or working with Learning Services to make up the work he had missed. He chose to stay in school and complete the work.

With much effort, dedication, and sobriety, Steve was able to finish the semester in good standing and with respectable grades. I think Steve was fortunate that he had people around him that cared, and that he was willing to take responsibility for the changes that needed to happen in his life. I have also seen students who choose not to accept responsibility and ultimately experience varying degrees of personal failure.

It is critical to have a good working relationship with the counseling center on campus, the academic deans, and professors. Nothing can replace or quantify the importance of everyone working together. I firmly believe the immediate success Steve experienced was the direct result of everyone communicating and working toward a common goal: Giving a young man back his life.

MEDICATION ISSUES

By the time a student enters college, he/she knows whether ongoing use of medication is necessary for enhanced concentration, reduced impulsivity, and decreased hyperactivity. Once away from the watchful eyes of parents or guardians, the college student must define the extent to which medication is necessary.

I have met very few people who actually enjoy taking medication needed for AD/HD. In fact, most adolescents resent that they have to take a “drug” to perform at a specific level. This resentment may result in the student opting to not continue their previous medication regime. Learning Service Coordinators can simply ask if the student is currently on medication. If they say “no”, probe to see if they were taking medication prior to attending the institution.

If students report that they were on medication prior to attending the school, and are now using medication irregularly or not at all, exploring the reasons for the discontinued use is important. If the student feels that he/she wants to finally do it “on their own” without the “crutch” of medication, reviewing the biophysical aspects of AD/HD is important.

If students insist on foregoing medication, invite them to participate in a two- week experiment. Have them chart their progress for one week on medication and off the next week. Thus, you can make the college environment the laboratory in which the student can “discover” what choice is to be in his/her best interest. I have found this to be particularly helpful. It creates an opportunity for the student to become responsible for his/her own knowledge surrounding the effects of taking and not taking medication.

CONCLUSION

If our college students feel prized and capable, there is a distinct probability that they will continually make choices in their best interest. Granted, they may experiment with substances or other risk-taking behavior. However, they will hopefully recognize when they have run a stop sign and make choices in the future to avoid the same mistake. Our children with special learning needs must be in an environment that plays to their strengths, and requires a significant amount of personal responsibility and accountability.

Often, students with special learning issues are thrown into the deep-end and expected to not only swim, but demonstrate Olympic-level style. College is a wonderful venue for our children with AD/HD to flourish and experience extraordinary levels of personal success. There must be a support structure in place that they can access if need be. In conclusion, the voice of a college senior seems to sum up the essence of what I have been trying to say:

> **When I got to college, I had this feeling that finally I could do what I wanted without someone analyzing my behavior or attitude. Admittedly I haven't been the easiest kid to parent or teach. I occasionally had beer in high school, but when I got to college, man, I just went hog wild. Heavy on the social, and light on the academics. I also enjoyed the feeling of drinking - a lot. My first year, I majored in partying and socializing. Needless to say, it all caught up with me, it always does. I had to take a year off from school. My grades were so pathetic that the only school that would take me as a student, besides community college, was one of the best schools in Virginia which I had been suspended from. My parents took a firm stand with me and said if I wanted to live at home, I had to take courses at the local community college and work full-time. If I wanted to go back to school, I knew what I needed to do. I've been successful since returning. I have also grown a great deal. I do believe that having a greater degree of preparation for school would have helped at some level. I really didn't know what to expect. Alcohol took over as the number-one priority. It was nice being able to numb-out and not worry. Having AD/HD has been a source of anxiety for me.**
>
> **Since coming back to school, I have taken advantage of some resources which help with studying, scheduling, and the like. Again, it would have made a huge difference If I used this in the beginning. Really though, I did not think a lot about these services once I started school. I guess using the services was never really impressed upon me. They have been great, and I feel gratitude for their help.**

References

Feldman, S. Denhoff, E., & Denhoff, J (1979).The attention disorders and related syndromes: Outcomes in adolescence and young adult life. In L. Stern & E.Denhoff (Eds.), *Minimal brain dysfunction: A developmental approach.* New York: Masson.

Satterfield, M., Satterfield, B., and Schell. (1987). Therapeutic interventions to prevent delinquency in hyperactive boys. *Journal of the American Academy of Child and Adolescent Psychiatry. 26:* 56-64.

Weiss, G., & Hechtman, L. (1993). *Hyperactive children grown up. (2nd ed.)* New York: Guilford Press. □

ACADEMIC COPING STRATEGIES IN COLLEGE STUDENTS WITH SYMPTOMS OF AD/HD

Patrick Turnock M.S., L.S.W.
Department of Psychology
Colorado State University

Untreated Attention Deficit Hyperactivity Disorder has been widely implicated in academic difficulty and failure among elementary and secondary school students. While the effect of AD/HD on postsecondary achievement has not been closely studied, evidence suggests that students with AD/HD continue to struggle in college. This study attempts to identify strategies with which academically successful AD/HD students may compensate for their symptoms of inattention, impulsivity and/or hyperactivity. Survey results from 151 university undergraduates indicate that students with many symptoms of AD/HD (High Symptom/HS group) used significantly less coping behavior than their low-symptom peers (Low Symptom/LS group). Moreover, while intelligence was associated with academic achievement among HS students, use of coping behavior was not. The opposite pattern was found for the comparison group. Coping strategy—but not intelligence—was significantly related to academic success among LS college students. Implications of these findings and directions for future research are discussed.

INTRODUCTION

While adults with symptoms of AD/HD struggle by definition, across a variety of settings (APA, 1994), Mannuzza and colleagues (1991) have noted that the nature of AD/HD symptoms makes the school environment particularly aversive. For example, Weiss, Hechtman, Milroy and Perlman (1985) found in their 15-year followup study of children with AD/HD, that fewer than five percent of the adults with AD/HD had completed college, compared to more than 40 percent of their non-AD/HD peer group. Other studies indicate significant impairments in emotional and psychosocial functioning among AD/HD students in college (Litfin, 1996; Ramirez, 1996; Slomkowski, Klein, & Mannuzza, 1995).

While little is currently known about the prevalence or effect of AD/HD in the university setting, clinicians suggest a positive educational outcome for some AD/HD college students (Hallowell & Ratey, 1994; Nadeau, 1994; Quinn, 1993). In separate long-term studies following AD/HD children into young adulthood, Mannuzza and colleagues (1993; 1997) found that 12% and 15% of their AD/HD samples, respectively, had completed a bachelor's degree. Perhaps as some investigators have hypothesized, a subset of AD/HD students successfully cope with their symptoms and achieve a measure of academic success (Faigel, 1995; Hallowell & Ratey, 1994; Heiligenstein and Keeling, 1995; Kaplan and Schachter, 1991; Nadeau, 1994; Quinn, 1993). If true, then it's possible that AD/HD students struggling academically can learn mechanisms of coping with their disorder which could help them do better.

This study will examine whether academic success among college students with symptoms of AD/HD is associated with greater use of academic coping strategies. The research hypothesis predicts that adult college students with symptoms of AD/HD demonstrating academic success differ from their less successful counterparts in the amount and/or type of academic coping strategies used to circumvent AD/HD symptoms interfering with competent school performance.

Table 1:

Research Questions
1) Do HS and LS college students* differ in academic success as measured by college GPA?
2) Are there any interactions among AD/HD symptom status, college GPA and/or gender in the use of coping skills?
3) Which coping strategies or combinations of coping strategies are most predictive of academic success for HS students? Are these different for LS students?

* "HS" and "LS" indicate "High-Symptom" and "Low-Symptom" adults, respectively, and refer to individuals in this study who reported having either many or few symptoms of AD/HD as described in DSM-III-R. These designations are described more fully in the methods section.

METHOD

Participants

One hundred, fifty-one students enrolled in Introductory Psychology classes at a large university (22,000) in the western United States participated in this study. Ages of the research participants ranged from 16 to 33 years, with a median age of 18 years. Ninety percent of the participants were identified as Caucasian; 1% were Black; 3% were Asian; 3% were Hispanic; and 3% marked the "other" category of racial identification. Eighty-eight (58%) participants were female; 30 were in the high-symptom (HS) group. Sixty-three subjects (42%) were male; 37 of them HS. Of the 67 HS students, 28 (42%) demonstrated high academic success during the semester in which they were participants, by scoring at or above the median grade point average for all subjects. The other 39 (58%), achieved a semester GPA below the sample median, thus achieving low academic status. Ten (15%) of the HS students reported having been previously "officially diagnosed as having Attention Deficit-Hyperactivity Disorder."

Measures

Symptomatology was measured according to Barkley's (1991) 18-item Adult AD/HD Symptom Checklist. Cut off scores were ten or more symptoms, and four or fewer symptoms for the HS and LS groups, respectively. Academic success was determined based on each participant's official grade-point average (GPA) for the semester during which they participated in the study, and their cumulative GPA one year later. Academic coping strategies were measured using two different instruments: the Coping Strategies Measure (CSM), developed for this study, and Brown and Holtzman's (1965) Survey of Study Habits and Attitudes (SSHA).

Categories of coping methods included: avoiding procrastination (e.g., "I do not begin a task until time pressure forces me to do so"); time management (e.g., "I schedule my time"); study methods (e.g., "I check over my answers before turning in my examination paper"); social support (e.g., "I seek support from friends or family when I am having problems"); and self-control (e.g., "I pursue only the types of tasks that I enjoy"). Previous research indicates that intelligence tends to significantly co-vary with measures of academic success (Fischer, Barkley, Fletcher, & Smallish, 1993; Lambert, 1988). Therefore, the Wonderlic Personnel Test (Wonderlic, 1988) was administered as a brief measure of cognitive ability.

Procedure

Fifteen-hundred students were screened for participation on the basis of the Brief Symptom Screening Form (BSSF), based on the *DSM-III-R* (APA, 1987). Those who indicated the presence of at least ten of eighteen AD/HD symptoms on the BSSF were eligible for inclusion in the HS group. Students indicating the presence of four or less symptoms on the BSSF were further screened for inclusion in the low-symptom (LS) control group. Final assignment to HS and LS groups was dependent on responses to the diagnostic measures found in the subsequent questionnaire packet each research participant completed.

RESULTS

Differences in Academic Success

LS students achieved significantly higher grades than the HS students. The mean semester GPA for the LS group was 2.89; the mean semester GPA for the HS group was 2.46. Similar mean differences were found for cumulative GPA (2.85 for LS; 2.36 for HS).

Differences in Coping Strategies

Students in the HS group scored significantly lower on a variety of coping strategy scales including: Avoidance of Procrastination; Self-Control Behaviors; and Study Methodology. Additionally, increased use of a coping strategies measure - Avoidance of Procrastination - was associated with higher grades, but only for LS students.

Among LS students, those with low grades procrastinated significantly more than the LS students with high grades. The same was not found for HS students, however. No significant difference existed in the amount of procrastination between the high-GPA, HS group and the low-GPA, HS group.

Gender

Gender differences contributed to two significant findings in this study. First, differences on the Social Support Scale indicated that college women in this study tended to seek and experience a greater level of social support than did men. Second, the result on the Time- Management Coping Scale showed that women reported significantly more time-management behavior than did men.

Multiple Regression Analysis

For the HS group, the IQ measure had a significant, positive correlation with both semester and cumulative GPA. This finding is consistent with that of other studies. For the LS group, however, the correlation between IQ and academic success was not significant.

Two separate, stepwise, multiple regression analyses were conducted to determine which predictors (the coping strategy measures and IQ) were most highly associated with the GPAs of college students. One analysis was conducted using only HS subjects, while the second included LS subjects.

For the HS students, analysis indicated that only IQ was a significant predictor of GPA. Not surprisingly, HS individuals with higher IQs also achieved higher grades. The Time Management Coping Subscale approached but did not reach, statistical significance in predicting semester GPA (p=.0552).

When HS students who were no longer enrolled at the university at the time of data analysis (2 semesters later) were dropped from the analysis, association between IQ and GPA for the remaining HS students became even stronger (from Adj. R2 = .071 to .163).

For LS subjects, the analysis indicated that Avoidance of Procrastination was the only significant predictor of GPA. LS students who avoid procrastination also achieve higher grades. For these students, IQ was not an important predictor of academic success.

FURTHER ANALYSIS

Additional results of interest in this study relate to several descriptive statistics. Numerous researchers previously have reported that AD/HD occurs in males two to nine times more often than in females (Barkley, 1988; Barkley, 1990; Biederman, 1991). It was surprising, then, to find that women comprised over 45% of the HS research group in this study.

Another interesting finding relates to dropout rates among subjects who participated in this research. Of the 151 subjects involved in this study, 67 were HS and 84 were LS. At the time of data analysis, roughly two semesters after this data was collected, 40 subjects had formally withdrawn from the university or had failed to register for classes for the semester. Twenty-seven of these students (68%), were from the high-symptom group, while 13 (32%) were from the low-symptom group. This difference in dropout rates between the HS and LS students is statistically significant. Stated another way, 40% of high symptom subjects, compared to 15% of low-symptom subjects dropped from the university rolls in the year after this data was collected.

Another statistic that may warrant attention involves the number of high-GPA versus low-GPA individuals in each symptom level group when looking at semester GPA and cumulative GPA. During the semester in which general psychology was taken, LS students surpassed HS students academically. While 59% of the students in the LS group achieved a GPA at or above the median for the entire sample (i.e., 2.80), only 41% of HS students had GPA's at or above average. When considering the overall GPA one year later, the percentage of the LS group considered successful (at or above the median GPA for the sample) was 61%, while the percentage of successful HS students had dropped to 32%. This finding was also statistically significant.

DISCUSSION

The intent of this study was to isolate factors contributing to success for individuals with AD/HD symptoms. It was expected that HS students, who had "run the gauntlet" by successfully navigating high school, and met entrance requirements for a four-year university, would have done so by employing academic coping strategies. Study results, however, show that college students with symptoms of AD/HD use fewer coping behaviors than their non-AD/HD peers. HS students approach studying in a less-organized, less-methodical way. They procrastinate considerably more, and employ fewer self-control, self-disciplinary behaviors. Academic success of

HS students had no relationship to their use of coping strategies. Intelligence was the only variable that predicted success among these HS students.

Academic Failure among HS Students

HS students achieved significantly lower grades, and dropped out of classes significantly more often than their LS counterparts. Present findings suggest that trends of higher-than-average school failure and dropout rates among students with many AD/HD symptoms, continue at the university level. It appears that the rate of failure may continue to increase for HS students already in college, as the success rate for these students declined significantly over the course of one year, while the rate for LS students remained virtually unchanged.

This finding may indicate an important and alarming trend for students with symptoms of AD/HD. The psychological and economic costs of their disorder may be severe. Failure to reach their academic and occupational potential may help explain why adults with AD/HD have higher rates of depression, lower self-esteem, and lower employment status than their non-AD/HD peers (Hechtman, 1991; Mannuzza, et al., 1993; Murphy, 1995a; Ratey, Greenberg, Bemporad, & Lindem, 1992; Slomkowski, Klein, & Mannuzza, 1995).

Individuals with symptoms of AD/HD may lack the capacities to ascertain the need for, and then to develop and implement strategies to cope with their symptoms. The notion that people with AD/HD are unable to develop and implement coping strategies because of deficits related to the AD/HD itself is supported by theories that describe the disorder as deficits in executive functions (Barkley, 1997; Denckla, 1993; Hallowell & Ratey, 1994; Nadeau, 1995; Quinn, 1995).

The executive functions of the brain are those that help people attend to, plan, organize, and control their behaviors. These include: attention; memory; organization; planning; initiation; self-inhibition; ability to change set; strategic behavior; and self-monitoring (Nadeau, 1995). Healthy executive functions permit goal-directed action and task persistence (Barkley, 1997).

Developing effective coping is a multifaceted and attention-demanding process of defining the problem; originating and initiating an appropriate strategy to cope with it; then carrying through on the new adaptive behaviors in a consistent fashion. Obviously, given the definition above, this process relies heavily on executive functions and therefore, presents special difficulties for those with deficiencies in these areas.

Just as deficient executive functioning can explain the failure of HS students to use academic coping mechanisms, poor self-monitoring and attention would be expected to impede effective self-diagnosis in this group. Similarly, other recent research suggests that the prevalence of AD/HD among college students may be considerably higher than previously thought (Heiligenstein & Keeling, 1995; Ramirez, 1996; Weyandt, Linterman, & Rice, 1995). Seen in this light, the finding that fewer than 15% of the HS group in the current study reported ever having been "officially diagnosed as having Attention Deficit-Hyperactivity Disorder", is not surprising.

Failure in behavioral execution of coping strategies, either at the point of initiation or at the stage of task persistence and follow-through, provides another example of compromised executive functioning.

Barkley (1997) has suggested that the problem for AD/HD individuals, is not a skill deficit, but rather a difficulty with behavioral execution. That is, HS students may possess knowledge of coping strategies effective for many people, and they may even have tried some of them out. Significant difficulty arises, however, in the consistent, appropriate application of these mechanisms. Because of deficiencies in executive functions, inhibited capacities for initiation, strategic behavior, or self-inhibition for completing activities or interests, may interfere with successful performance. If this is the case, as Barkley suggests, then point-of-performance interventions may provide a more effective course of action than would training in use of coping mechanisms.

An example of a **point-of-performance intervention** is the use by HS students of "coaching" organizations or individuals. Coaches, according to Hallowell (1995), provide a number of invaluable functions for the adult with AD/HD. These include organization and structure promote on-task behavior and provide encouragement. Goodwin and Corgiat (1992) reported significantly improved academic success in college student with AD/HD following an intensive point-of-performance and cognitive training intervention program.

Specific interventions in this case study included **environmental restructuring** (e.g. finding a quiet place to work); internal and external memory strategies (e.g. mnemonic devices; programmable wristwatch, dayplanner); and organizational study-skills aids. In combination with medication, repeated practice of these interventions until habitual reportedly decreased executive function deficits.

Other clinicians report favorable results from helping their adult AD/HD clients to develop effective coping strategies for school and work (Hallowell and Ratey, 1994; Kotwal, Burns, & Montgomery, 1996; Murphy, 1995b; Nadeau, 1994; Quinn, 1993). Kershner, Kirkpatrick and McLaren (1995) found that one highly successful adult with executive function deficits coped by surrounding himself with individuals whose abilities compensated for his limitations. Treatment successes such as these suggest that adults with AD/HD can, with focused and structured coaching, adopt adaptive behavioral strategies for coping with symptoms of AD/HD.

Gender

HS college students in this study demonstrated an approximately equal gender representation. While this appears to be incongruent with the results of numerous earlier studies, most previous research has been based on AD/HD children and adolescents (who generally are the same children followed up into adolescence). The few studies that have examined a cross-section of AD/HD adults support the finding of approximately equal prevalence of AD/HD among men and women (Biederman, et al., 1993; Biederman, et al., 1994; Murphy & Barkley, 1995).

Results from the present study suggest several possible explanations for the unexpected finding of nearly equal numbers of HS men and women. Use of two coping strategies significantly and consistently differentiated women from men. Women scored higher than men on the measure of time management. Chronically poor time management results in higher stress levels and/or a greater incidence of school failure for HS men relative to HS women. Additionally, women in this study reported that they pursued and experienced higher levels of social support than men.

Perhaps social support acts as a buffer against dropping out of school. No published research has, to date, examined this question with relation to individuals with AD/HD. Moreover, Mannuzza et al. (1993), reported that 25% of subjects with AD/HD do not complete high school. The authors do not mention what proportion of the students are male, suggesting by implication, that the percentage is as expected and only a small fraction, if any, are female.

CONCLUSION

Results of this study support the need to carefully reexamine some long-standing assumptions regarding incidence and treatment of AD/HD among college students. As knowledge and understanding of AD/HD in adult populations grow, and use of more sophisticated diagnostic tools and methods increases, a clearer picture of the problem and treatment options will emerge. Meanwhile, it appears as if the kinds of help typically offered to college students with symptoms of AD/HD (i.e., the teaching of compensatory skills) may not, in practice, be much help. Instead, the most practical kinds of aid for college students with AD/HD may provide structure, guidance and coaching - the "executive function" model of student-aid services.

References

American Psychiatric Association. (1987). *Diagnostic and statistical manual of mental disorders (Third Edition-Revised*). Washington, DC: Author.

American Psychiatric Association. (1994). *Diagnostic and statistical manual of mental disorders (Fourth Edition).* Washington, DC: Author.

Barkley, R.A. (1988). Attention deficit hyperactivity Disorder. In E. Mash & L. Terdal (Eds.), *Behavioral assessment of childhood disorders (2nd ed.,* pp. 69-104). New York: Guilford Press.

Barkley, R.A. (1990). *Attention deficit hyperactivity disorder: A handbook for diagnosis and treatment.* New York, NY: The Guilford Press.

Barkley, R.A. (1991). Patient's behavior checklist for AD/HD adults. In Barkley, R.A., *AD/HD workbook*. New York: Guilford Press.

Barkley, R.A. (1997). Behavioral inhibition, sustained attention and executive functions: Constructing a unifying theory of AD/HD. *Psychological Bulletin.*

Biederman, J. (1991). Attention deficit hyperactivity disorder (AD/HD). *Annals of Clinical Psychiatry, 3,* 9-22.

Biederman, J., Faraone, S.V., Spencer, T., Wilens, T., Mick, E., & Lapey, K.A. (1994). Gender differences in a sample of adults with attention deficit hyperactivity disorder. *Psychiatry Research, 53,* 13-29.

Biederman, J., Faraone, S.V., Spencer, T., Wilens, T., Norman, D., Lapey, K., Mick, E., Krifcher-Lehman, B., & Doyle, A. (1993). Patterns of comorbidity, cognition, and psychosocial functioning in adults with attention deficit hyperactivity disorder. *American Journal of Psychiatry, 150,* 1792-1798.

Brown, W.F. & Holtzman, W.H. (1965). *Survey of study habits and attitudes.* The Psychological Corporation, New York.

Denckla, M. B. (1993). The child with developmental disabilities grown up: Adult residua of childhood disorders. *Neurologic Clinics, 11*(1), 105-125.

Dooling-Litfin, J.K. & Rosen, L.A. (1997) Self-esteem in college students with a childhood history of attention deficit hyperactivity disorder. *Journal of College Student Psychotherapy, 11,* 69-82.

Faigel, H.C. (1995). Attention deficit disorder in college students: Facts, fallacies, and treatment. *Journal of American College Health, 43,* 145-150.

Fischer, M., Barkley, R.A., Fletcher, K.E. & Smallish, L. (1993). The adolescent outcome of hyperactive children: Predictors of psychiatric, academic, social and emotional adjustment. *Journal of the American Academy of Child and Adolescent Psychiatry, 32 (2),* 324-332.

Goodwin, R. E., & Corgiat, M. D. (1992, September-October). Cognitive rehabilitation of adult attention deficit disorder: A case study. *Journal of Cognitive Rehabilitation,* 28-35.

Hallowell, E. M. (1995). Psychotherapy of adult attention deficit disorder. In K. Nadeau (Ed.), *A comprehensive guide to attention deficit disorder in adults: Research, diagnosis, treatment* 146-167. New York: Brunner/Mazel.

Hallowell, E.M. & Ratey, J.J. (1994). *Driven to distraction: Recognizing and coping with attention deficit disorder from childhood through adulthood.* New York: Touchstone.

Hechtman, L. (1991). Resilience and vulnerability in long term outcome of attention deficit disorder. *Canadian Journal of Psychiatry, 36,* 415-421.

Heiligenstein, E. & Keeling, R.P. (1995). Presentation of unrecognized attention deficit hyperactivity disorder in college students. *Journal of American College Health, 43* (5), 226-228.

Kaplan, C.P. & Shachter, E. (1991). Adults with undiagnosed learning disabilities: Practice Considerations. Families in Society: *The Journal of Contemporary Human Services,* (April), 195-201.

Kershner, J., Kirkpatrick, T., & McLaren, D. (1995). The career success of an adult with a learning disability: A psychosocial study of amnesic-semantic aphasia. *Journal of Learning Disabilities, 28 (2),* 121-126.

Kotwal, D.B., Burns, W.J., & Montgomery, D.D.(1996). Computer-assisted cognitive training for AD/HD: A case study. *Behavior Modification, 20 (1),* 85-96.

Lambert, N.M., (1988). Adolescent outcomes for hyperactive children: Perspectives on general and specific patterns of childhood risk for adolescent educational, social, and mental health problems. *American Psychologist, 43* (10),786-799.

Mannuzza, S., Klein, R. G., Bessler, A., Malloy, P., & Hynes, M. E., (1997). Educational and occupational outcome of hyperactive boys grown up. *Journal of the American Academy of Child and Adolescent Psychiatry, 36, (9),* 1222-1227.

Mannuzza, S., Klein, R.G., Bessler, A., Malloy, P., & LaPadula, M. (1993). Adult outcome of hyperactive boys; Educational achievement, occupational rank, and psychiatric status. *Archives of General Psychiatry, 50,* 565-576.

Mannuzza, S., Klein, R.G., Bonagura, N., Malloy, P., Giampino, T.L., & Addalli, K..A. (1991). Hyperactive boys almost grown up. *Archives of General Psychiatry, 48,* 77-83.

Murphy, K. (1995a). Empowering the adult with ADD. In K. Nadeau (Ed.), *A comprehensive guide to attention deficit disorder in adults: Research, diagnosis, treatment* 135-143. New York: Brunner/Mazel.

Murphy, K. (1995b). *Out of the fog: Treatment options and coping strategies for adult attention deficit disorder.* New York: Hyperion.

Murphy, K. & Barkley, R.A. (1995). Norms for the DSM-IV symptoms lists for AD/HD in adults; Preliminary results. The *AD/HD Report, 3* (3), 6-7.

Nadeau, K. G. (1994). *Survival guide for col lege students with ADD or LD.* New York: Magination Press.

Nadeau, K. G. (1995). Life management skills for the adult with ADD. In K. Nadeau (Ed.), *A comprehensive guide to attention deficit disorder in adults: Re search, diagnosis, treatment* 191-217. New York: Brunner/Mazel.

Quinn, P. O. (Ed.). (1993). *ADD and the college student: A guide for high school and college students with attention deficit disorder.* New York: Magination Press.

Quinn, P.O. (1995). Neurobiology of attention deficit disorder. In K. Nadeau (Ed.), *A comprehensive guide to attention deficit disorder in adults: Research, diagnosis, treatment* , 18-31. New York: Brunner/Mazel.

Ramirez, C.A., Rosen, L.A., Deffenbacher, J.L., Hurst, H., Nicoletta, C., Rosencrantz, T., & Smith, K. (1997). Anger and anger expression in adults with high AD/HD symptoms. *Journal of Attention Disorders, 2,* 115-128.

Ratey, J.J., Greenberg, M.S., Bemporad, J.R., & Lindem, K.J. (1992). Unrecognized attention-deficit hyperactivity disorder in adults presenting for outpatient psychotherapy. *Journal of Child and Adolescent Psychotherapy, 2* (4), 267-275.

Slomkowski, C., Klein, R.G. & Mannuzza, S.(1995). Is self-esteem an important outcome in hyperactive children? *Journal of Abnormal Child Psychology, 23,* (3), 303-315.

Weiss, G. & Hechtman, L.T. (1993). *Hyperactive children grown up: AD/HD in chidren, adolescents, and adults.* Guilford Press: New York.

Weiss, G., Hechtman, L.T., Milroy, T., & Perlman, T. (1985). Psychiatric status of hyperactives as adults: A controlled 15-year follow-up of 63 hyperactive children. *Journal of the American Academy of Child Psychiatry, 24,* 211-220.

Weyandt, L.L., Linterman, I., & Rice, J.A. (1995). Reported prevalence of attentional difficulties in a general sample of college students. *Journal of Psychopathology and Behavioral As sessment, 17* (3), 293-304.

Wonderlic, (1988). *Wonderlic personnel test manual.* Wonderlic: Northfield, Illinois.

RETENTION INTERVENTIONS FOR COLLEGE STUDENTS WITH AD/HD

Anne McCormick, M.Ed.
Associate Director of Learning Services
American University

College retention programs serving students at risk can also meet the needs of students with AD/HD by offering an opportunity to succeed in all areas of their lives. Retention programming incorporates academic and personal growth opportunities in the campus community. Ancillary individualized services and accommodations that students with AD/HD require are included within this service delivery model. As college service providers evaluate and redesign programming to meet the needs of students with AD/HD, retention programs can meet the needs of students with AD/HD and utilize shared financial and programming resources of the university community.

INTRODUCTION

Since 1970, when the first postsecondary programs began for students with learning disabilities, their refinement and expansion has addressed the needs of students with learning disabilities and AD/HD, and have paralleled changing demographics and economic capabilities of students attending college.

These two factors were the catalysts for outreach and retention programming to attract and retain specific populations of students for whom college was not an option. Late-evening and weekend classes were offered for students who worked full-time; academic credit was given for life experience; and non-degree programs were designed as preparation classes for skills critical to academic success.

For service providers of students with learning disabilities and AD/HD, this programming trend coupled with increasing numbers of students submitting documentation for AD/HD, has led to a reevaluation of the "first, individualized retention programs for at-risk students" begun in the 1970's.

Additionally, current research and growing clinical experience of college students with AD/HD, has proven that accommodations alone are not enough to enable them to succeed academically and personally in postsecondary education. Comprehensive programming, addressing the personal, social and academic needs of college students with AD/

HD has, in many cases, been the result of this evaluation process.

COLLABORATIVE PROGRAM APPROACH

However, such comprehensive approaches are not always financially feasible for many institutions when limited to a specific population of students, i.e., students with AD/HD. Collaboration with other student services providers on college campuses can provide retention programming and service components for students with AD/HD with an inclusive program model, and in a financially reasonable manner. Collaborative programming models result in overall student satisfaction, retention, and ultimately, graduation. "Institutions and students would be better served if a concern for the education of students, their social and intellectual growth, were the guiding principle of institutional action. When that goal is achieved, enhanced student retention will naturally follow", (Tinto, 1993).

Although collaborative programming may be a fiscally responsible approach for programming students with AD/HD, it requires service providers to work outside the special education paradigm that previously guided the original design and implementation of programming for college students with learning disabilities and AD/HD. The components of retention programming continues original programs for students with learning disabilities and AD/HD, but from a more inclusive approach. The model puts "students' needs and interests squarely at the center ... wrapping programs and services around the student, rather than requiring that an individual student's needs be manipulated so they might fit the system." (Noel, Levitz & Saluri, 1985).

Retention programming addresses the personal, social, and academic needs of students through orientations, advising, learning and academic support, counseling, and other collaborative student support models. This holistic approach to serving students is based on the overall college student departure statistics that, "less than 15 percent of all students departures from college result from academic failure.", (Tinto, 1987).

Programming and individualized support for students with AD/HD must be performance-based, and extend to all aspects of the student's life. Retention programs can provide the necessary basis for students with AD/HD to succeed.

ADJUSTMENT TO COLLEGE

The challenge faced by moving programs for students with AD/HD into the mainstream is that the roots of college adjustment problems for these students are inherent in their disability. Their risk factors are multiplied, and they are hypersensitive to the personal and social factors which may overwhelm college adolescents.

College students with AD/HD are least able to screen out the incredible overflow of factual and experiential information imbedded in the experience. Although involvement in college life is recommended to create a sense of community, involvement is another risk factor for college students with AD/HD. They have difficulty limiting their activities, focusing on the task at hand, and completing their academic requirements. In college, the impulsivity of AD/HD becomes the nemesis of their disability, for it negatively impacts on executive functioning. This is the" locus of control" which college students in general are exercising for the first time.

Formerly, parents were the locus of control, and in college, it is up to the student to find and exercise his/her own self-control. A successful college student has found his/ her internal command center and can maintain it through will and executive control. For college students with AD/HD, this executive control center is hidden under symptoms of their disability, and requires extra support to maintain a healthy balance of priorities in their college life. Retention programs offer a command center that channels student's interests through structured opportunities, such as community service, and provide an informal coaching network of academic counselors, advisors, and peer mentors.

Though for many disability service providers, the best way to address manifestations of AD/HD may be the original individualized service model, current needs of institutions dictate that a collaborative model be adopted. Collaborative retention programming contributes to a student's academic success through enhancing his/her overall satisfaction with the campus community and the overall institution. It promotes an environment in which students can achieve success in **all** areas of their lives.

"The more students learn; the more they sense they are finding and developing a talent; the more likely they are to persist. Reenrollment or retention is not then the goal Retention is the result or by-product of improved programs and services in our classroom and elsewhere on campus that contribute to student success". (Noel, 1985).

COMPONENTS OF RETENTION PROGRAMS

Student Factors

Factors that promote goals of academic success must be at the student and institutional level. At the student level, programming must offer a challenge and a support student's investment of time and energy. For students with AD/HD, the return must be timely and tangible. Recognition by peers through peer-mentor components of retention programming, as well as individual academic counseling sessions with staff and faculty, contribute to this timely and tangible return.

Results of retention programs are student involvement and satisfaction. For students with AD/HD, channeling their strengths through the academic pursuit rather than in other areas of their life, is critical. This can best be addressed through the one-on-one academic counseling component in conjunction with program elements for strong retention programming.

Institutional Factors

Institutional factors that contribute to academic success are not only seen in the quality of academic instruction, but in the scope of this instruction. Freshmen seminar courses are important links for ensuring student success. These are important not only from the standpoint of course content in key academic success strategies, but also in content which addresses the classic deterrents to academic success: procrastination and poor time management.

Freshman Seminar Courses

For students with AD/HD, freshman seminar courses provide group reinforcement for study strategies which they are addressing in one-on-one sessions with service providers. The **Freshman Seminar Course** should meet as a regular class; as an offering of an academic department. It should teach academic survival skills, from study and reading strategies to writing a research paper.

Even strong high school records do not prepare students for the rigors of postsecondary education. For students with AD/HD, the freshman seminar course offers another model of support for the transition to college. Identification with peers who may be like the student with a disability, aids in their satisfaction and increases motivation to succeed.

Orientation

Another institutional factor that contributes to academic success is **orientation.** Orientation is an opportunity to be integrated into an already existing community. "Because the most dependent learners are those at entry into college, academic and student support services should be concentrated most heavily in the freshmen year. Intrusive, proactive strategies must be used to reach freshmen with these services before they have an opportunity to experience feelings of failure, disappointment and confusion," (Noel, 1985).

Two factors contributing to the failure of students with AD/HD are the challenges of transitioning in general, and years of accumulated damage to their self-esteem. Separate orientations, which are blended into an overall orientation provide, students a peer group and, "an edge" to bolster their sense of self when the rest of the students arrive.

For students with AD/HD, this could not be more important. In fact, requiring orientation for at-risk students can provide the bridge, and coupled with the semester-long freshman seminar, offer ego reinforcement throughout the semester.

Peer-mentor Model

When orientation is done in collaboration with other student services, an added benefit for students with AD/HD is the peer-mentoring model. It develops naturally and can provide an umbrella over programming and one-on- one instruction.

One alarming symptom of adolescent AD/HD is social immaturity. Their social immaturity, often results in increased at-risk behaviors. Peer-mentor programs are critical in turning negative influences into positive ones. Peer mentors can be the most influential relationships students make. "Generally, students tend to change their values, behaviors and academic plans in the direction of the dominant orientation of their peer group," (Astin. 1993). For an able college student with AD/HD, peer mentors provide the social and psychological support needed for personal success.

When peer mentors are trained in listening and counseling skills, they can provide, in effect, the coaching function for students with AD/HD. Although, service providers recognize the importance of a "coach," fiscal realities may not provide for it. Service providers cannot provide the comprehensive service that a coach can. A study buddy, for example, is a concrete motivator for a student who needs help getting started on the task and completing it. However, students keep quite different hours from their service providers, and peer mentors are more likely to meet a student schedule. A mentor can also give advice which is more respected when given by a peer.

Advising

Advising is another key institutional factor supporting students with AD/HD. For students with AD/HD, the process of registration presents a challenge. Course scheduling and selection should be carefully monitored to ensure success for the student. Though students may view taking all evening classes as an opportunity to have more time, students with AD/HD may not use that time effectively. Not only is timing of classes important, but the number of courses or course load is also.

A reduced course load balanced by a job on campus may be ideal for students with AD/HD. The more structure from outside sources, such as classes, and jobs, the better for these students who have not yet developed their locus of control.

Continuity of advising is another important element in providing services. Though many institutions are moving toward a one-stop, one shop model for advising, one-on-one advising should still be an option for selected populations of students, i.e., students with disabilities. Students with AD/HD cannot always complete a task within a certain time frame. They are unable to screen extraneous information and other sensory information. Large group instruction and procedures must be supported in individual sessions with an academic counselor.

CONCLUSION

Retention programs with the above components provide a way to "integrate, not isolate, the academic and social experiences of students," (Tinto, 1987). The need for integration into the college student mainstream is of paramount importance for students with AD/HD. Frequently, students with AD/HD do not accept their disability and subsequently harbor anger about it and education in general. Their social immaturity may add to their sense of rebellion.

Weaving students with AD/HD into the broader academic community, with students, staff, faculty lessens the negative feelings related to self and education. Retention programs provide students with AD/HD a second chance at achieving academic and personal success within the mainstream.

From an institutional perspective, there is a cost benefit to retention programs for students at risk. Collaboration with program experts in student development, and learning specialists in academic enhancement programs, meets individual student needs in a cost-effective model. Though service providers for students with disabilities have before focused primarily on accommodations, we now have a more comprehensive approach that meets student and institutional needs.

As we learn more about AD/HD and its effects on college students, we must affirm the challenge these students face and highlight their successes within the university community. " Colleges and universities are like other human communities; that student departure, like human communities generally, reflects both the attributes and actions of the individual and those of the other members of the community in which that person resides," (Tinto, p.5). Retention programs for students with AD/HD recognize student's individuality and include them in the university community.

References

Astin, A.W. *(1993). What matters in college: Four critical years revisited.* San Francisco: Jossey-Boss, Inc.

Noel, L., Levitz, R., Saluri, D., & Assoc. *(1985). Increasing student retention: Effective programs and practices for reducing the dropout rate. Jossey-*Boss, Inc.

Tinto, V. (1993). *Leaving college: Rethinking the causes and cures of student attrition. (2nd edition).* Chicago: The University of Chicago Press.

☐

THE ISSUE OF MEDICATION FOR COLLEGE STUDENTS WITH AD/HD AND RELATED DISORDERS

Patricia O. Quinn, M.D.
Clinical Assistant Professor of Pediatrics
Georgetown University

Psychotropic medications, particularly stimulants, are considered to be the most useful tools available for dealing with AD/HD and its related disorders. While medication alone does not cure the disorder, it certainly can reduce many of its symptoms. This article examines the use of medication at the postsecondary level, linking responsibility to this usage. Effective strategies for addressing side effects and the rational for combination therapy will also be discussed.

INTRODUCTION

For many years, it has been widely postulated that Attention Deficit/Hyperactivity Disorder (AD/HD) has a neurobiochemical basis. However, it is only over the last decade that convincing evidence has been produced of both structural and functional abnormalities in areas of the brain responsible for attention and executive functioning. These areas are known to contain dopamine pathways, thereby further linking that neurotransmitter to neurological dysfunction.

Stimulants remain the medications of choice for appropriate treatment of this disorder. Current research further indicates that seventy percent (70%) of individuals with AD/HD continue to display symptoms affecting functioning into early adulthood. However, at this developmental stage, medical management can be a tricky business.

To ensure success at college, all students with AD/HD need to address their disorder and take charge of an appropriate treatment regime including medication. The service provider can assist the student in becoming more knowledgeable about medications, and facilitate the process of his/ her obtaining appropriate health care on campus. Delivery of health care services for these students will be discussed more fully in the next article by Paul Steinberg. But first, I would like to present information that I feel each student should be aware of regarding his/ her medication as they address issues related to AD/HD.

These facts will be presented in a format that service providers are encouraged to use when working with students with AD/HD who are on medication for that disorder. Permission is therefore given to reproduce this information.

FACTS FOR COLLEGE STUDENTS REGARDING MEDICATION FOR AD/HD

1. Know the name of your medication and how it works. Ritalin (methylphenidate) and Dexedrine or Adderall (amphetamines) are the most commonly prescribed medications for ADD/AD/HD. Ritalin and Dexedrine are available as either short-acting (usually 4 hours) and longer-acting (6-12 hours) preparations. Short-acting medications take effect in 20 minutes while long-acting mediations may take up to an hour to be fully effective. Both medications work on correcting the neurobiochemistry of the brain thought to be the cause of the symptoms seen in AD/HD. These medications enhance brain receptor functioning, inhibit breakdown of certain neurotransmitters in the brain, and can themselves act as false transmitters.

2. If you needed stimulant medication to concentrate in high school, you most likely will need medication to concentrate in college. Stimulants are the treatment of choice for AD/HD. They increase concentration and focus while decreasing distractibility and impulsivity. Approximately seventy percent (70%) of individuals with AD/HD continue to have problems with attention throughout their lifespan.

3. Stimulants improve cognitive functioning but you will still have to put in time studying and attending classes. Taking medication before classes can help you concentrate and enhances information gathering. You can also use your medication dosage times to establish a schedule for studying. You should know how long your medication will be effective and therefore determine how much focused study time you have available. Set up a schedule for studying accordingly and stick to it.

Stimulants can also help you stay focused while you are reading and thus improve your reading comprehension. Students frequently report that they read all of the materials assigned, but have no clue as to what they have just read because they weren't paying attention. To solve this problem be sure your stimulant medication is in effect while you are reading.

4. AD/HD affects all aspects of life: social, home, athletics, and employment. As you probably already know, one doesn't just need to concentrate and be focused in class. You also need to focus on what your friends are saying, or to instructions on the job. Focus and concentration are important in sports whether you are playing tennis or catching a football. Often being distracted and/or acting impulsively can get you in trouble with your friends or (when you are driving) with the law. Therefore, it is important for you to assess how much the symptoms of your AD/HD affect your functioning, and to take your medication accordingly. Improved concentration may improve the quality of your life in many ways.

5. It is important to take medication as prescribed for you by your physician. Don't self-medicate. Many students have a mistaken notion that if one pill works well, two pills will work better. While this may be true for some other medications, that is not the case with stimulants. For them, there is something called the **"window of efficacy"**. This term refers to the amount of medication that is the most effective for your particular brain chemistry. The amount of medication you need does not depend on body weight or on the severity of your symptoms, but rather on what works for you. That is why you may need to periodically reassess if your medication is still functioning at optimum effectiveness.

Many students come to college on the same dose of medication that worked for them in elementary or high school. That's fine if that determination has been made after a recent, careful review of your needs and is demonstrated by the continued effectiveness of that particular dosage level.

6. It is illegal to distribute (share) your prescription medication. Stimulant medications are controlled substances. The law states that all medications should be kept in their original container and labelled with your name, and name and dosage of the medication inside. It is important not to transfer your stimulant medication to another bottle for any reason.

It is against the law for you to distribute a controlled substance. This means not sharing your medication with a friend who needs to study for that big test or concentrate in class or a sport. Many students carry their medications with them at all times to avoid leaving them unattended in their rooms, where they may be more accessible to others.

7. Drugs and alcohol do not mix with stimulants. Your AD/HD is caused by a chemical imbalance in your brain. You are taking stimulant medication to try to correct that imbalance. If you use other drugs such as marijuana which also affect brain dopamine, you wreak havoc with an already imbalanced system. Your medications will not be as effective and you will be more impaired in your functioning. Taking stimulants also affects the metabolism of alcohol in the body, and can result in higher blood alcohol levels, thus increasing the risk of alcohol poisoning. Mixing cocaine and the stimulants can kill!

8. Checkups are important. Check in with the health center on campus when you arrive and monthly after that. As a controlled substance, stimulant prescriptions need to be refilled monthly. When you arrive on campus, it is important for you to visit the health center and set up a mechanism to receive your medication prescriptions regularly. If you depend on other systems, they may break down at some point and you may be left without medication. This usually occurs at critical times like before a test, during study for finals, or during exams. It is also important for the staff to become familiar with you, so that if questions arise about dose or side effects, they can be answered more readily. You can also have your weight checked monthly, to make sure that you are getting enough calories and not losing weight, because you are not hungry or forget to eat.

9. See your primary physician at least once a year for an examination and blood tests if necessary. As with all chronic conditions and medications that are taken routinely, it is important to have a regular checkup. Blood tests that assess liver functioning are important if you are on certain medications. Your physician back home is likely the one that diagnosed your AD/HD and knows you the best. Be sure you check in with him or her from time to time to assess how things are going.

These facts are taken from *RE-THINKING AD/HD: A Guide for Fostering Success in Students with AD/HD at the College Level,* edited by Patricia Quinn and Anne McCormick, Advantage Books (888-238-8588), Bethesda, MD, 1998.

COMMON MEDICATIONS USED TO TREAT AD/HD

The following tables provide information for service providers and students about the various stimulant and non-stimulant medications used for the treatment of AD/HD and their duration of action.

STIMULANTS

Methylphenidate (Generic)

Ritalin	5,10, and 20 mg tablets; effects lasts 3-5 hours
Ritalin SR	20 mg sustained-release; (should not be cut or broken); lasts 6-8 hours

Dextroamphetamine

Dexedrine	5 and 10 mg tablets; lasts 3-5 hours
DexedrineSpansules	5,10,15mg; lasts 6-10 hours
Adderall (Combination of dexedrine salts)	5, 10, 20, 30 mg (long acting); 8 -12 hours

Pemoline

Cylert	18.75, 37.5, 75 mg tablets; Initially takes 2 weeks to take effect. Lasts 12-24 hours. Not a first-line medication. Others should be used first. **May cause liver dysfunction.**

NONSTIMULANTS

Clonidine

Catapres	0.1, 0.2, 0.3 mg; lasts 8-12 hours
Catapres TT	1,2,3, patches; lasts 5 to 7 days

Guanafacine

Tenex	1.2 mg tablets; lasts 8-12 hours

Bupropion

Wellbutrin	75, 100 mg tabs; Takes effect in several days.

Antidepressants may also be used in certain circumstances to treat either AD/HD or related symptomatology. Except for the tricyclic antidepressants (TCA's), they do not address the primary symptomatology of inattentiveness and distractibility.

ANTIDEPRESSANTS

Tricyclics (TCA's)

Imipramine	10, 25, 50, 75 mg tabs; Takes 5-10 days to take effect. Lasts 12-24 hrs.
Desipramine	10, 25, 50, 75 mg tabs; Takes effect 3-5 days; Lasts 12-24 hours.

Selective Serotonin Reuptake Inhibitors (SSRIs)

Prozac	10, 20 mg pulvules; Initially takes 2-4 weeks to take effect. Has a half-life of several days.
Zoloft	25, 50, 100 mg tablets; Takes a week or 2 to initially take effect. Half-life of 24 hrs.
Paxil	20, 30 mg tablets; Initially takes 2-3 weeks to take effect. Has a half-life of 14 hours.

COMORBID CONDITIONS AND THE REQUIREMENT FOR COMBINED THERAPY

While stimulants are 75 to 86% effective in addressing the symptoms of inattention, distractibility, and impulsivity, a significant number of students with AD/HD also have comorbid symptomatology. This leads us to the need for combination therapy to address all issues facing a student with AD/HD.

Other medications such as the antianxiety medication, wellbutrin, or the anticonvulsant, tegretol, also have been used to treat severe symptoms of AD/HD or in cases that do not respond to stimulant medication. As AD/HD frequently occurs with other conditions, it may be necessary for a physician to prescribe several medications at one time to treat all of the symptoms that a student is exhibiting. In those cases, finding the right combination of medication is extremely important. However, individuals should not be given medications just to counter side effects of a medication currently administered. In those cases, side effects should be examined or a change in medication should be considered.

EFFECTIVELY ADDRESSING SIDE EFFECTS

Side effects of medications can often be problematic and the main reason for a student to discontinue his/her treatment. Service providers can be influential in assisting the student in properly identifying side effects and taking steps to individually address them. When dealing with this problem, it is important to independently identify the side effect causing the student difficulty. Encouraging the continuance of the medication regime prescribed, if it is successful in reducing the symptoms of AD/HD, while simultaneously addressing the side effect, usually proves successful in most cases.

The following list contains some of the most common symptoms encountered by individuals on the previously mentioned medications and suggests various ways for eliminating or at least reducing them. It should be noted that this list is not meant to be a substitute for medical treatment when necessary. The student should always be urged to contact his/her physician to discuss specific side effects and suggestions for addressing them.

SIDE EFFECTS COMMON TO STIMULANTS

Decreased appetite - The student should be encouraged to eat at regular intervals, preferably prior to taking medication or after it has worn off. High-calorie food choices should be encouraged if weight loss or poor weight gain is an issue. Increasing regular exercise may also improve appetite.

Stomachaches and/or headaches - These are commonly due to not eating before taking medication or skipping meals while their medication is in effect because they are not hungry. Both symptoms are usually relieved by eating.

Insomnia - The student should be made aware that he/she will normally not be able to sleep while stimulant medication is in effect. They should thus plan dosage schedule and amount of stimulant medication taken accordingly. If a medication lasts 4 hours, they will not be able to take it at 10 p.m. and expect to fall asleep at midnight.

A decrease in late evening doses, and an increase in regular exercise may also help here. If insomnia is a significant presenting symptom, and not related to stimulant dose, a physician should be contacted to discuss the possibility of adding clonidine at bedtime.

Irritability - Students who report this side ef fect should watch their caffeine intake and decrease it accordingly. If irritability is occurring as medication wears off, a change to a longer-acting preparation or an overlapping of doses may prove beneficial. Some students report irritability on methylphindate and d o not have this same response to amphetamines. In these cases, the prescribing physician should be consulted to determine if such a switch in stimulants may alleviate this symptom.

Tics - If involuntary motor movements should occur while a student is on medication, a physician should be consulted to determine the best course of action. In some cases, changing medications or the addition of clonidine may be useful in decreasing these movements. Keep in mind that while stimulants may increase tics, they do not cause them.

Depressed mood or social withdrawal - All students should be carefully monitored for the onset of symptoms of depression. If these side effects do occur while on stimulants, the student should contact the prescribing physician for reevaluation of current medication and/or the need for addition of an antidepressant medication to the current regime.

ANTIDEPRESSANT SIDE EFFECTS

Sedation and/or fatigue - This side effect will usually gradually decrease over time as the student gets used to taking medication. Taking the medication at bedtime may also be helpful.

Dry mouth or dizziness - Make sure that the student is aware that he/she should drink plenty of liquids.

Gastrointestinal distress - Taking medication after meals or an increase in fiber may help this symptom.

Nervousness/tremor/increased anxiety - The student should be encouraged to contact his/her physician if these symptoms are reported.

The student should also be urged to contact his/her physician if an increase in hyperactive or manic behaviors, severe insomnia, or a rash, are reported while taking any SSRI. Service providers should also be aware that sudden deaths have been reported during the use of desipramine, and that all students taking that medication should be monitored with an EKG prior to starting the medication and with any increase in dose. Students taking tricyclic antidepressants should be cautioned about increasing the prescribed dose of medication on their own.

CAFFEINE AND EXERCISE

Here I would like to say a few words about caffeine and exercise. In working with many high school and college students, I have found that during this period they begin to complain that their medication makes then too irritable and jittery. This usually is found not to be a side effect of their stimulant medication, but rather the result of increased caffeine consumption. The student forgets that his/her medication is a stimulant and that caffeine in coffee, iced tea, cola beverages, and chocolate enhance that effect. Students should be encouraged to decaffinate themselves by drinking caffeine-free beverages.

Over the years working with some very hyperactive students, I have found that recommending a daily exercise workout can be very effective in increasing their ability to settle down to concentrate or study and in decreasing hyperactivity and restlessness. If a student does not play an organized sport, I recommend that they make use of the sports facilities on campus and run, swim, play tennis, or do another type of aerobic workout daily. These students report feeling calmer and generally have a better mood and outlook. Many students run or exercise just prior to study periods, while others report that they need to stretch and/or exercise after sitting for long periods. Some students exercise prior to settling down for the night.

USING MEDICATION DOSAGE SCHEDULE TO PROVIDE DAILY STRUCTURE

Using a medication regime that focuses on the duration of action of the medication can also help by providing the structure that leads to the development of a workable daily schedule for students. Students with AD/HD should be encouraged to group their classes together as a "block" (not longer than 3 1/2 hours) at the time of day that they function at their best (e.g. morning, afternoon, or evening). Most stimulants last at least 3-4 hours, by setting up such a daily schedule, the student can then take medication prior to this "block" of classes.

The student should also be encouraged to use this line of thinking to set up "blocks" of study time. Taking medication and knowing that they will have 3 - 4 hours of effective focus for study and/or reading causes students to begin to schedule their day into "blocks" around medication. This process has gone on to lead to a whole new way of thinking of and dealing with AD/HD symptoms with the student eventually taking responsibility for both his/her medication and other life activities.

References

Barkley, R.A., DuPaul, G.J., & McMurray, M.B. (1991). Attention deficit disorder with and without hyperavtivity: Clinical response to three dose levels of methyphenidate. *Pediatrics, 87,* 519-531.

Barkley, R.A., McMurray, M.B. Edelbrock, C.S., & Robbins, K. (1990). Side effects of methyphenidate in chidren with attention deficit hyperactivity disorder: A systemic, placebo-controlled evaluation. *Pediatrics, 96,* 184-192.

Barrickman, L., Noyes, R. Kuperman, S, Schumacher, E. & Verda, M. (1991). Treatment of ADHD with fluoxetine: A preliminary trial. *Journal of the American Academy of Child and Adolescent Psychiatry, 30,* 762-767.

Biederman J. (1991). Sudden death in children treated with a tricyclic antidepressant. *Journal of the American Academy of Child and Adolscent Psychiatry, 30,* 495-498.

Gammon, G.D., & Brown, T.E. (1993). Fluoxetine and methyphenidate in combination for treatment of attention deficit disorder and comorbid depressive disorder. *Journal of Child and Adolescent Psychopharmacology, 3,* 1-10.

Hunt, R.D., Arnstein, A.F., & Asbell, M.D. (1995). An open trial of guanfacine in the treatment of attention deficit hyperactivity disorder. *Journal of the American Academy of Child and Adolescent Psychiatry, 34,* 50-54.

Nehra, A. Mullick, F., Ishak, K.G., & Zimmerman, H.J. (1990), Pemoline-associated hepatic injury. *Gastroenterology, 99,* 1517-1519.

Quinn, P.O. (1997). *Attention deficit disorder: Diagnosis and treatment from infancy to adulthood.* New York: Brunner/Mazel.

Wilens, T.E., & Biederman, J. (1992). The stimulants. *Pediatric Psychopharmacology, 15,* 191-222.

□

MEETING THE HEALTH CARE NEEDS OF STUDENTS WITH AD/HD ON CAMPUS

Paul Steinberg, M.D.
Associate Director, Counseling and Psychiatric Service
Georgetown University

When meeting the medical needs of students with AD/HD, college campuses both improve their retention rates and enhance the quality of life for their students with AD/HD. With help from learning specialists, any associated learning disabilities can be assessed with reasonable accommodations provided. Physicians, particularly psychiatrists, can assess and treat other comorbid conditions including depression, mood swings, and obsessive-compulsive disorder. Medical providers face a dilemma in ensuring that all students with AD/HD get diagnosed and treated while preventing dissemination of stimulant medications to students without the disorder.

INTRODUCTION

Over the past decade, college campuses across the country have reported a major increase in demand for evaluations by physicians and learning specialists for attention-deficit disorder. Students, parents, professors, tutors and learning specialists are more aware of the possibility of AD/HD. Media attention to AD/HD has allowed more students to recognize the possibility of AD/HD and thus come in on their own.

In addition, many extremely bright students may "hit a wall" academically in college, after compensating reasonably well in the less rigorous academic environment of high school. They come to the attention of professors, tutors, and learning specialists. Some students may have been diagnosed earlier in school with a vague attentional problem, but their parents were reluctant to let him/her follow through with a medical evaluation and possible medication. Reaching college, however, these same students may wish to try medication on their own despite their parents' reluctance. Heightened awareness of AD/HD and this desire for treatment have meant that AD/HD is not as underdiagnosed as it was five to ten years ago. Critics contend that presently this condition may be overdiagnosed, but there is no evidence to support that conclusion. Instead, clinicians may be better at diagnosing students correctly. Unlike the situation of many recently diagnosed parents, who express regret that diagnosis and treatment was unavailable when they were younger, the diagnosis is now being made in high school and college.

MEDICAL PERSONNEL NEEDS

Growing awareness of AD/HD, and its impact on student retention and academic performance, has demanded a shift in medical personnel needs on college campuses. No campus can truly manage without some access to a physician, preferably a psychiatrist, who can assess AD/HD and its comorbid conditions and provide appropriate treatment. Campus health services must seek to employ physicians, who are trained in the treatment of AD/HD and knowledgeable about prescribing medications and addressing side effects.

CONFIRMING THE DIAGNOSIS

Clearly the diagnostic process may often begin with the alert response of a learning specialist. One open to the possibility of a previously undiagnosed attention-deficit disorder in students with difficulties reading, writing, or notetaking. After careful historytaking by the learning specialist or physician, the next step is a subject of controversy and debate: Should educational testing be required of the student? In fact, testing can give confirmatory indications suggestive of AD/HD but may not be truly "diagnostic".

One may suggest that perhaps educational testing can be reserved for students with an accompanying learning disability in addition to their AD/HD. In fact, for these students, treatment for AD/HD should precede the educational testing so that learning deficits attributable to AD/HD will not muddle the picture. It may be quite unrealistic to test all students with AD/HD, although results of many standardized tests like the LSAT's and MCAT's seem to suggest a need for educational testing. However, with mandatory educational or psychological testing, AD/HD might become a "rich man's diagnosis" and students with minimal financial resources would again become underdiagnosed.

COMORBID CONDITIONS

Several comorbid conditions, often accompanying AD/HD, have created a need for input from a psychiatrist knowledgeable about AD/HD, or, at the very least, a psychologically attuned physician. Pediatricians because of their training may be especially attuned to these aspects of AD/HD.

Significant mood swings are a common condition associated with AD/HD. Joseph Biederman, M.D., in Boston, has noted that as many as 20 percent of adolescents with AD/HD may go on to develop full-blown bipolar illness. According to the current state of knowledge, the areas of the midbrain (the caudate and globus pallidus) which mediate attention may also be a relay-station for moods; for thoughts and obsessions; for learning; and for motor activity and tics.

Accordingly, AD/HD may be accompanied by not just mood swings and depression, but also by obsessive-compulsive disorder (often mild), learning disabilities, and motor tics. Medications such as methylphenidate may exacerbate any of these conditions. For example, some students may experience an enhanced irritability, sadness, and even depression as the effects of stimulant medication wear off. Occasionally physicians may need to treat depression or mood swings before any AD/HD medication is initiated: A knowledge of antidepressants and mood stabilizers is, therefore, essential.

COMBINING SERVICES

At many colleges and universities, the college counseling center is housed in the same space as the learning services center.

Connection of the two services has often been somewhat incidental allowing for a sharing of administrative staffs and for economies of scale. Interestingly, colleges are now finding that there is a true functional rationale for combining these two services.

With the need for diagnosing AD/HD becoming so great, close association of learning specialists, psychiatrists and psychologists becomes essential. In fact, in Washington, D.C., four major universities have their learning services closely associated with their counseling center: American University, Catholic University, Georgetown University, and the University of Maryland. This arrangement allows for a close coordination between learning specialists who may first become aware of the AD/HD, the educators and psychologists who may do some diagnostic testing, and prescribing physicians.

MEDICATION ISSUES

Abuse Potential

On college campuses or wherever the diagnosis and treatment of AD/HD are undertaken, however, one major dilemma remains prominent - How does one make sure that each individual with AD/HD gets appropriate treatment (allowing students a level academic playing field) while avoiding the risk of distributing stimulants (methylphenidate and/or amphetamines) to others who wish to use these drugs recreationally?

Some college health services end up over-controlling methylphenidate and dextroamphetamine prescriptions. In the process, they may provide less than optimal care for their students with AD/HD. Other centers, may be too loose in the prescribing these controlled substances, and the medications may get into the hands of students who do not have AD/HD. One myth demanding to be shattered is that students with AD/HD might be abusing medications prescribed for them. On the contrary, it is extremely rare for a student with AD/HD to be abusing stimulants (methylphenidate or other amphetamines). In fact, students with AD/HD almost invariably describe that the "stimulant" medications slow them down.

Stimulant medications help students **with** AD/HD follow through with their intentions to study. While medicated, they can ignore stimuli which would otherwise draw them away from unstimulating reading or writing assignments. But heightened capacity to follow through with intentions is not a pleasant sensation for students with AD/HD. Medication takes them away from their usual pleasant state of responding to multiple stimuli at any one time. Accordingly, when students with AD/HD have no intention of studying, for example, going out with friends on a weekend evening, the last substance they would want in their systems would be an amphetamine. In contrast, students **without** AD/HD find that methylphenidate and dextroamphetamine can be significant stimulants.

On many college campuses students have crushed up illicitly obtained methylphenidate and snorted it to get a "high". Unfortunately, students with AD/HD may be involved in illicit distribution of these medications. They may sell or give away extra or unused medications. Sometimes, they report that fellow students have stolen their medication. Physicians and students need to report these activities to campus police or even to the Drug Enforcement Agency . Without a concerted effort on the part of students with AD/HD and their prescribing physicians in halting these abuses, physicians may end up prescribing only noradrenergic medications, such as desipramine and buproprion, for treatment of AD/HD. Such a move would be a major loss.

Eating Disorders

Might students with eating disorders, who also have AD/HD, become abusers of methylphenidate and dextroamphetamine? These medications clearly produce suppression of appetite - a desirable effect for students with weight and body-image concerns. To get this desired loss of appetite, however, students would have to take these medications around the clock without any breaks in their dosage schedules. (Students often note that when the medication is out of their systems, they have a compensatory hunger and increase in appetite) . But an around-the-clock regimen would create some unpleasant sensations for students at times when they aren't interested in working and studying. Nevertheless, an eating disorder accompanying AD/HD requires full assessment.

Marijuana and Illicit Drug Use

Many students with AD/HD, especially those previously undiagnosed, may have used or abused other drugs before or after reaching college. Students often report that marijuana has helped to slow down their thought processes and has helped them to ignore competing, attractive stimuli and thoughts. Fortunately, methylphenidate and dextroamphetamine work significantly better than marijuana in treating AD/HD. However, these students may have already become addicted to marijuana's remarkable capacity to help its users "care less". Should a clinician still prescribe amphetamines for a student who appears to be a daily marijuana user?

This is a difficult decision, made more difficult by the probability that marijuana in its own right may be interfering with the "intention" of studying. But, if a clinician is certain that the student has AD/HD based on a longstanding history confirmed by parents and grade-school teachers, then the benefits of methylphenidate and similar medications which allow the student to focus and study, may provide incentive for that student to seek help for substance abuse.

Likewise, students may have been attracted to cocaine and illicit amphetamines to help slow them down. The diagnosing of AD/HD and the prescribing of methylphenidate or dextroamphetamine in these cases may provide significant relief and reassurance.

PSYCHIATRIC CARE

Clearly, students with a prior history of illicit drug use or abuse, require close follow-up. They may require other treatments including possibly 12-step programs. Similarly, AD/HD students who have associated Obsessive-Compulsive Disorder (OCD) or depression and mood swings, require further psychiatric care. In general, students with AD/HD have seen their self-esteem plummet over the years, especially while undiagnosed. They may have been teased and taunted for being "stupid" or "lazy", or at best "spacey", by family members and peers. Consequently psychotherapy may be crucial in turning around this low self-esteem.

PHYSICIAN FOLLOW-UP

Students with uncomplicated AD/HD need brief monthly or bimonthly visits with a physician or psychiatrist. (For some students, a month's supply of medication, the limit for "controlled" substances, may last for several months when used only as needed for study, classes, etc.). During these visits, continued efficacy and side effects of medication should be discussed; dosage schedules, problem areas, and contraindications reviewed; and appropriate adjustments made. Weight check and blood testing may also be performed.

CONCLUSION

It is hoped that when all of these proposed medical and educational resources are potentially available on a college campus, retention rates for students with AD/HD may become significantly higher. In the past, students with AD/HD had notoriously low-retention rates in college. Even now, in presumably more enlightened times, some colleges are balking at the idea of admitting students who have learning needs, despite these students' often-remarkable intellectual talents.

These resources, to be sure, are not inexpensive. But the many capabilities of students who have AD/HD - and their special capacity to act quickly (perhaps "impulsively") and spontaneously, without much thinking - add considerably to the diversity of a college campus. Just as importantly, with the treatments now available, students with AD/HD may live a fuller, richer life on campus. They no longer have to study in a highly inefficient, unfocused way. Instead, they are able to study, read, write, and learn much more efficiently and have time, finally, for a potentially guilt-free personal life. Medical and psychiatric services must therefore be available on campus to help them achieve their goals. □

LEGAL ISSUES REGARDING AD/HD AT THE POSTSECONDARY LEVEL

Peter S. Latham, J.D., and Patricia H. Latham, J.D.
Partners, Latham & Latham, and Founders,
National Center for Law and Learning Disabilities

Disability service providers at postsecondary institutions may best serve their institutions and students if they have a basic knowledge of the Rehabilitation Act of 1973, the Americans with Disabilities Act of 1990, and of the pertinent regulations and case law developments. It is important to be familiar with AD/HD and other impairments covered under the law: the legal test for when an impairment is a disability - substantially limited in a major life activity, the concept of being otherwise qualified for the program; accommodations required under the law; and requirements for professional documentation of a disability. This article provides an overview of these issues.

INTRODUCTION

The law's Constitutional concepts of due process and equal protection are applied to individuals with disabilities and made specific by two Federal statutes: The Rehabilitation Act of 1973 (RA),(29 U.S.C.§ 791 et seq.), and the Americans with Disabilities Act of 1990 (ADA) (42 U.S.C. § 12101 et seq.).

The RA made discrimination against individuals with disabilities unlawful in three areas: 1] employment by the executive branch of the Federal government ; 2] employment by most Federal government contractors; and, 3] activities which are funded by Federal subsidies or grants. This latter category includes all public elementary and secondary schools and most postsecondary institutions.

The statutory section which prohibits discrimination in grants was numbered § 504 in the original legislation. The RA is often referred to simply as "Section 504". Other sections, for example, create a limited requirement for affirmative action in the hiring of individuals with disabilities by the executive branch of the Federal government and most Federal government contractors.

In 1990, Congress enacted the ADA. This Act extended the concepts of 'Section 504 of the RA to: 1] employers with 15 or more employees (Title I); 2] all activities of state and local governments, including but not limited to employment and education, including public postsecondary institutions (Title II); and, 3] virtually all places which offer goods and services to the public- termed "places of public accommodation," including private postsecondary institutions (Title III). Virtually all postsecondary institutions are covered by the ADA, except for religiously controlled schools.

LEGAL PRINCIPLES

The RA and ADA have created the right to be free from discrimination based on one's disability in all but a few postsecondary institutions, - i.e., all but institutions that are religiously controlled and accept no Federal funds. The protections of these laws extend to those who: 1] are individuals with disabilities under the law; 2] are otherwise qualified, with or without a reasonable accommodation; 3] are being excluded from employment or education solely by reason of their disability; and, 4] are covered by applicable federal law. These laws require that institutions make their programs accessible to individuals with impairments, including ADD, that substantially limit a major life activity. The concepts of: impairment; substantially limits; major life activity; and otherwise qualified, are explored below.

Protections of the RA and ADA apply only to an "individual with a disability" which is any individual who:

> (i) has a physical or mental impairment which substantially limits one or more of such person's major life activities;
> (ii) has a record of such an impairment; or,
> (iii) is regarded as having such an im pairment. [29 U.S.C. § 706(8)(B).]

The second and third definitions are intended to protect individuals who: 1] previously had a disability but do not now; or, 2] are treated as though they had a disability but do not. The most important category for our purposes is the first, and it is discussed below. The ADA contains definitions which are "equivalent" to those contained in the RA. The discussion which follows applies to both statutes unless otherwise specified.

IMPAIRMENTS COVERED

The definition of a "physical or mental impairment" includes: "any mental or psychological disorder, such as mental retardation, organic brain syndrome, emotional or mental illness, and specific learning disabilities," 29 CFR § 1613.702(b)(2). Note that "specific learning disabilities" are expressly covered by the regulations. The courts have indicated that they will utilize the definition of a "specific learning disability" as it appears in the IDEA, when construing this regulation. (Argen v. New York State Board of Law Examiners, 860 F. Supp. 84 (S.D.N.Y. 1994).

ADD is not specifically mentioned in the regulations. ADD, however, has been recognized as a "mental or psychological disorder" by the U. S. Department of Education's Office for Civil Rights. In Letter of Findings, (LOF) OCR Docket No. 04-90-1617; 17 Sep 90; Gaston County School District the OCR ruled that the Gaston County School District of North Carolina (which received federal funding) failed to identify, evaluate, and provide to a child with ADD, a free public education appropriate to his disorder and thereby violated the RA. (29 U.S.C. § 794).

There are similar holdings in the private school and employment setting. In Bercovitch v. Baldwin School, Inc., Docket No. 97-1739 (1st Cir. Jan.12, 1998), the Court held, among other things, that AD/HD is an "impairment" within the meaning of both the RA, and ADA. In Davidson v. Midelfort Clinic, Ltd.; Docket No. 96-2860 (7th Cir. January 7, 1998), the Court found that ADD is "a chronic psychological disability resulting from a biochemical imbalance" and therefore, an "impairment" under the ADA. Thus, ADD is an impairment. The next question in individual cases is whether or not ADD substantially limits a major life activity.

SUBSTANTIALLY LIMITS

The impact of the impairment must be substantial. Regulations provide that the term "substantially limits" means that an individual is: 1] "unable to perform a major life activity that the average person in the general population can perform"; or, 2] is "significantly restricted as to the condition, manner or duration" of performing the major life activity in question, when measured against the "average person in the general population." [29 CFR ¶¶ 1630.2(j)(1)(i)-(ii)] The meaning of "substantially limits" in the context of professional licensing cases will be discussed in depth in Section 4 of this article.

MAJOR LIFE ACTIVITIES

An impairment must substantially limit a major life activity before it can be considered a "disability" under the law. The major life activities are considered to be: caring for oneself; performing manual tasks; walking; seeing; hearing; speaking; breathing; learning; and working. [29 CFR ¶ 1630.2(i)] The Equal Opportunity Employment Commission (EEOC) recognizes as major life activities: thinking, concentrating, and interacting with others.

One court has recognized reading as such an activity. Note that the regulations provide that learning and working are major life activities, and these are the ones that most concern us. However, working is treated differently from all other major life activities for purposes of considering whether an individual with an impairment is substantially limited.

In order to determine whether a substantial limitation on working exists, the individual's impairment must bar him or her from significant classes of jobs, and not just a particular job. Only disabilities with the former (and broader) impact are considered substantially to limit working.

OTHERWISE QUALIFIED

For coverage under both RA and ADA, an "individual with a disability" must be one who is "otherwise qualified." An "otherwise qualified" individual is one who, though possessed of a disability, would be eligible for the education or job with or without a reasonable accommodation. The institution or employer must either provide the accommodation or justify the refusal to provide it. (Fitzgerald v. Green Valley Area Education Agency, 589 F. Supp. 1130 (S.D. Iowa 1984). The application of these legal principles to postsecondary education is discussed below.

POSTSECONDARY EDUCATION

Under RA and ADA, postsecondary institutions must make accessible to individuals with disabilities, programs including courses and examinations. However, institutions are not required to make modifications in courses or examinations that would alter the essential nature or constitute an undue hardship on the institution.

The evolving case law is providing guidance as to whether or not an individual is a qualified individual with a disability and what accommodations are required.

TYPES OF ACCOMMODATIONS

Accommodations, often termed auxiliary aids and services, are required by RA and ADA to be made available to students with

ADD and other disabilities, who need these accommodations in order to access the institution's courses, examinations and activities. Accommodations may include: extended test time; individual room for test; taped examinations; large-print examinations; large-print test answer sheets; qualified readers; transcribers; interpreters; taped texts; and other similar accommodations, aids and services.

Alternative arrangements may be utilized, including videotaped lectures, cassettes and prepared notes. The governing principle is that methods of instruction provided to the student with ADD or learning disabilities must be "effective" in achieving "contemporaneous communication" of the "educational experience, among all participants in a manner that can be understood by each individual", and that allows for "equal participation in the educational experience" offered by the institution. (United States v. Becker C.P.A. Review, CV 92-2879 (TFH) D.D.C. 1994). These must be provided at no extra charge to the student. (University of Arizona, Letter of Findings (LOF) OCR Docket No. 09-91-2402; 2 NDLR ¶ 285; United States v. Board of Trustees for the University of Alabama, 908 F.2d 740 (11th Cir. 1990).

Specific accommodations that are generally required where documentation supports the need in particular cases include: extended test time; individual room for tests; and the other accommodations listed above.

Specific accommodations that may not always be legally required include: foreign language waiver or course substitution, and mathematics waiver or course substitution. Educational institutions that can justify the need for mastery of a foreign language in a particular program, would be able to require such mastery. Otherwise, the institution could be required to allow the course substitution. (Guckenberger et al. v. Boston University et al.; C.A. No. 96-11426-PBS, (D. Mass. August 15, 1997).

Specific accommodations that generally are not legally required include: (1) modification in type of test, e.g., short answer rather than multiple choice, and more pointed questions rather than open-ended questions; (2) extended time on a practical exercise, such as for giving a physical exam in physician's assistant program; and, (3) extended time to complete the practical part of a program, such as three years to complete the two-year clinical part of medical school.

Accommodations, aids, and services that focus on increasing the skill level of the student in the area of the disability are not required by the ADA and the RA. For example, an institution would not be required to provide developmental reading courses or remedial tutoring services free-of-charge to a student with dyslexia. (Halasz v. University of New England, 816 F. Supp. 37 (D. Me. 1993).

Institutions may offer separate programs (which may include separate courses and services), for students with learning disabilities, provided that qualified students are clearly informed that they have a choice between : a) the separate program, and, b) regular programs offered with suitable modifications and auxiliary aids at no additional charge. Institutions may limit students to entry into separate programs only if these students are truly not qualified for regular programs offered with suitable modifications and auxiliary aids at no additional charge.

LIMITATIONS ON THE DUTY TO ACCOMMODATE

A postsecondary institution has no obligation to provide accommodations which will alter the fundamental nature of the course materials or course of study being offered. (Wynne v. Tufts University School of Medicine, 976 F.2d 791 (1st Cir. 1992). (See also Pandazides v. Virginia Board of Education et al., 946 F.2d 345 (4th Cir. 1991). Nor does such an institution have an obligation to provide accommodations which will result in an economic hardship to the institution.

Economic hardship is measured by the impact on the institution's financial resources, not its relationship to the size of the requesting student's tuition. For this reason, few institutions argue that accommodations will produce an economic hardship. Institutions generally have no duty to identify students with disabilities, but rather to respond to disclosure of a disability and requests for specific accommodations.

PROFESSIONAL LICENSING

Cases in the professional licensing area may have ramifications for postsecondary institutions. A number of recent cases have explored why individuals in professional school with a record of academic accomplishment may be "substantially limited", and thus individuals with disabilities.

Price v. The National Board of Medical Examiners , Civil Action No. 3:97-0541; (S.D. W.VA. 06 June 1997), considered the request of three medical students who had no history of substantial academic difficulties, but who had been diagnosed by responsible professionals as having learning disabilities and/or ADD, for an injunction requiring additional time on the United States Medical Licensing Examination (USMLE), Step 1.

The Court ruled that the students were not individuals with disabilities under the ADA because their impairments did not limit their academic performance when compared to most people. The Court described the medical students thus:

> First, each plaintiff has some learning difficulty. Second, each of the students has a history of significant scholastic achievement reflecting a complete absence of any substantial limitation on learning ability. Further, this record of superior performance is corroborated by standardized test scores measuring cognitive ability and performance. Finally, there is a complete lack of evidence suggesting that plaintiffs cannot learn at least as well as the average person. That is, these students do not suffer from an impairment which substantially limits the life activity of learning in comparison with most people.

Based on these findings, the Court concluded that the medical students were not protected under the ADA.

In Bartlett v. New York State Board of Law Examiners, et al.; 970 F. Supp. 1094 (S.D.N.Y. 1997), (Bartlett I), a law school graduate with a Ph.D. in Educational Administration, sought and obtained the following reasonable accommodations on the New York Bar Examination: 1) "double time over four days"; 2) "the use of a computer"; 3) permission to circle multiple choice answers in the examination booklet"; and, 4] large print on both the New York State and Multistate Bar examinations". The Court found that Bartlett suffered from "a learning deficit", which takes the form of an "inability to read as well as the average law student".

Consequently, this deficit substantially limits her in the major life activities of test-taking and working because it operates to bar her from an entire class of jobs: the practice

Index

Appendix

Diagnostic Criteria for Attention Deficit/ Hyperactivity Disorder

A. Either (1) or (2):

(1) Inattention: six or more of the following symptoms that have persisted for at least the last six months

(a) often fails to give close attention to details or makes careless mistakes in schoolwork, work , or other activities

(b) often has difficulty sustaining attention in tasks or play activities

(c) often does not seem to listen when spoken to directly

(d) often does not follow through on instructions and fails to finish schoolwork, chores, or duties in the workplace (not due to oppositional behavior or failure to understand directions

(e) often has difficulty organizing tasks and activities

(f) often avoids, dislikes, or is reluctant to engage in tasks the require sustained mental effort (such as schoolwork or homework)

(g) often loses things necessary for tasks or activities (e.g. toys, school assignments, pencils, books, or tools)

(h) is often easily distracted by extraneous stimuli

(i) is often forgetful in daily activities

(2)**Hyperactivity-impulsivity:** six or more of the following symptoms that have persisted for at least the last six months

Hyperactivity

(a) often fidgets with hands or feet or squirms in seat

(b) often leaves seat in classroom or in other situations in which remaining seated is expected

(c) often runs about or climbs in situations in which it is inappropriate (in adolescents or adults, may be subject to feelings of restlessness)

(d) often has difficulty playing or engaging in leisure activities quietly

(e) is often "on the go" or often acts as "driven by a motor"

(f) often talks excessively

Impulsivity

(g) often blurts out answers before questions have been completed

(h) often has difficulty awaiting turn

(i) often interrupts or intrudes on others (e.g., butts into conversations or games)

B. Some hyperactive-impulsive or inattentive symptoms that caused impairment were present before age 7 years

C. Some impairment from the symptoms is present in two or more settings (e.g., at school [or work] and at home)

D. There must be some clear evidence of clinically significant impairment in social, academic, or occupational functioning

E. The symptoms do not occur exclusively during the course of a Pervasive Developmental Disorder, Schizophrenia, or other Psychotic Disorder and are not better accounted for by another mental disorder (e.g., Mood Disorder, Anxiety Disorder, Dissociative Disorder, or a Personality Disorder).

Reprinted with permission from the Diagnostic and Statistical Manual of Mental Disorders, Fourth Edition. Washington, DC, American Psychiatric Association, 1994.

of law. In other words, the impact of Bartlett's learning disability was not compared to the average member of the population. Rather, her impairment was measured against the ability of the average law student. Essentially, the Bar Examination was viewed as an employment test.

In this ruling, the Court found Bartlett entitled to these accommodations because time is not essential on the bar examination. "Given that defendants admit that they grant accommodations to persons with various types of disabilities, they are stopped from arguing that the bar examination is intended to test either reading or the ability to perform tasks under time constraints." (Op. at 78] In any event, "the visual ability to read, and the ability to perform tests under time constraints are not 'essential functions' of a lawyer." (Op. at 78). In short, the Bar Examination is purely a test of knowledge for which time is irrelevant. Hence, in the Court's view, the granting of accommodations does not lower standards. As we go to press, the case is on appeal.

No doubt, there will be continuing developments in this area of law. Whatever standard is ultimately adopted for determining substantial limitation, it seems clear that thorough documentation of the disability will continue to be essential.

DOCUMENTATION

Most documentation involves three steps: diagnosis; evaluation of impact; and recommendations. Together, they establish : 1.) the existence of a disability; 2.) the areas of functioning affected by that disability; and, 3.) the specific accommodations required because of that disability.

How much documentation is enough?

The ADA addresses the question of documentation in connection with academic and license testing. The Preamble to Regulation on Nondiscrimination on the Basis of Disability by Public Accommodations and in Commercial Facilities, which provides guidance on the proper interpretation of the ADA and its implementing regulations, provides that : 1) "requests for documentation must be reasonable"; 2) "must be limited to the need for the documentation or aid requested"; and, 3) the "applicant may be required to bear the cost of providing such documentation...." (28 C.F.R. § 36; App. B; Preamble to Regulation on Nondiscrimination on the Basis of Disability by Public Accommodations and in Commercial Facilities, pp. 614, 615) (Emphasis added).

If the documentation submitted by a student is insufficient to establish a disability and/ or entitlement to a requested accommodation, the institution may request additional documentation, and, if the documentation continues to be insufficient, the institution may decline to provide the accommodation.

CONCLUSION

The RA and ADA mandate that reasonable accommodations be provided individuals with disabilities, e.g., those individuals whose impairments such as LD/AD/HD, limit substantially one or more of that person's major life activities. Reasonable accommodations are often called auxiliary aids and services. They must be extended in the areas of admissions testing, the delivery of course materials, and in nonacademic areas of campus life. ☐

A more thorough discussion of the law and documentation requirements, including cases decided under the RA and ADA, is contained in two books by the authors of this chapter: *Attention Deficit Disorder and The Law* and *Documentation and The Law*, JKL Communications, P.O. Box 40157, Washington, DC 20016.